REGENTS RENAISSANCE DRAMA SERIES

General Editor: Cyrus Hoy
Advisory Editor: G. E. Bentley

THE TWO NOBLE KINSMEN

JOHN FLETCHER

and

WILLIAM SHAKESPEARE

The Two Noble Kinsmen

Edited by
G. R. PROUDFOOT

UNIVERSITY OF NEBRASKA PRESS · LINCOLN

Publishers on the Plains

MANUFACTURED IN THE UNITED STATES OF AMERICA

Regents Renaissance Drama Series

The purpose of the Regents Renaissance Drama Series is to provide soundly edited texts, in modern spelling, of the more significant plays of the Elizabethan, Jacobean, and Caroline theater. Each text in the series is based on a fresh collation of all sixteenth- and seventeenth-century editions. The textual notes, which appear above the line at the bottom of each page, record all substantive departures from the edition used as the copy-text. Variant substantive readings among sixteenth- and seventeenth-century editions are listed there as well. In cases where two or more of the old editions present widely divergent readings, a list of substantive variants in editions through the seventeenth century is given in an appendix. Editions after 1700 are referred to in the textual notes only when an emendation originating in some one of them is received into the text. Variants of accidentals (spelling, punctuation, capitalization) are not recorded in the notes. Contracted forms of characters' names are silently expanded in speech prefixes and stage directions, and, in the case of speech prefixes, are regularized. Additions to the stage directions of the copy-text are enclosed in brackets. Stage directions such as "within" or "aside" are enclosed in parentheses when they occur in the copy-text.

Spelling has been modernized along consciously conservative lines. "Murther" has become "murder," and "burthen," "burden," but within the limits of a modernized text, and with the following exceptions, the linguistic quality of the original has been carefully preserved. The variety of contracted forms (*'em, 'am, 'm, 'um, 'hem*) used in the drama of the period for the pronoun *them* are here regularly given as *'em*, and the alternation between *a'th'* and *o'th'* (for *on* or *of the*) is regularly reproduced as *o'th'*. The copy-text distinction between preterite endings in *-d* and *-ed* is preserved except where the elision of *e* occurs in the penultimate syllable; in such cases, the final syllable is contracted. Thus, where the old editions read "threat'ned," those of the present series read "threaten'd." Where, in the old editions, a contracted preterite in *-y'd* would yield *-i'd* in modern spelling (as in "try'd," "cry'd," "deny'd"), the word is here given in its full form (e.g., "tried," "cried," "denied").

Punctuation has been brought into accord with modern practices. The effort here has been to achieve a balance between the generally light pointing of the old editions, and a system of punctuation which, without overloading the text with exclamation marks, semicolons, and dashes, will make the often loosely flowing verse (and prose) of the original syntactically intelligible to the modern reader. Dashes are regularly used only to indicate interrupted speeches, or shifts of address within a single speech.

Explanatory notes, chiefly concerned with glossing obsolete words and phrases, are printed below the textual notes at the bottom of each page. References to stage directions in the notes follow the admirable system of the Revels editions, whereby stage directions are keyed, decimally, to the line of the text before or after which they occur. Thus, a note on 0.2 has reference to the second line of the stage direction at the beginning of the scene in question. A note on 115.1 has reference to the first line of the stage direction following line 115 of the text of the relevant scene.

CYRUS HOY

University of Rochester

Contents

List of Abbreviations

Bertram	P. Bertram. *Shakespeare and "The Two Noble Kinsmen."* New Brunswick, 1965.
Brooke	C. F. Tucker Brooke, ed. *The Shakespeare Apocrypha.* Oxford, 1908.
Chappell	W. Chappell. *Popular Music of the Olden Time.* 2 vols. London, 1855–1859.
Child	F. J. Child. *The English and Scottish Popular Ballads.* 5 vols. Cambridge, Mass., 1882–1898.
Colman	G. Colman, ed. *The Dramatic Works of Beaumont and Fletcher.* Vol. X. London, 1778.
conj.	conjecture
corr.	corrected
Dyce	A. Dyce, ed. *The Works of William Shakespeare.* 2nd ed. Vol. VIII. London, 1866.
Dyce 1846	A. Dyce, ed. *The Works of Beaumont and Fletcher.* Vol. XI. London, 1846.
F	Beaumont and Fletcher, second folio, 1679.
Herford	C. H. Herford, ed. *The Two Noble Kinsmen.* London, 1897.
Knight's Tale	G. Chaucer. "The Knight's Tale." F. N. Robinson, ed. *The Complete Works of Geoffrey Chaucer.* 2nd ed. Cambridge, Mass., 1957.
Kökeritz	H. Kökeritz. "The Beast-Eating Clown, *The Two Noble Kinsmen,* 3.5.151." *Modern Language Notes,* LXI (1946), 532–535.
Lamb	C. Lamb. *Specimens of English Dramatic Poets Who Lived about the Time of Shakespeare.* London, 1808.
Leech	C. Leech, ed. *The Two Noble Kinsmen.* New York, 1966.
Littledale	H. Littledale, ed. *The Two Noble Kinsmen.* London, 1876, 1885.

Mason	J. Monck Mason. *Comments on the Plays of Beaumont and Fletcher*. London, 1798.
OED	*Oxford English Dictionary*
punct.	punctuation
Q	Quarto, 1634
1711	*The Works of Mr. Francis Beaumont and Mr. John Fletcher*. Vol. VII. Printed for Jacob Tonson, London, 1711.
1750	*The Works of Mr. Francis Beaumont and Mr. John Fletcher*. Thomas Seward, John Sympson, and Lewis Theobald, eds. Vol. X. London, 1750.
Skeat	W. W. Skeat, ed. *The Two Noble Kinsmen*. Cambridge, 1875.
S.D.	stage direction
S.P.	speech prefix
Tilley	M. P. Tilley. *A Dictionary of the Proverbs in England in the Sixteenth and Seventeenth Centuries*. Ann Arbor, 1950.
uncorr.	uncorrected
Walker	W. S. Walker. *A Critical Examination of the Text of Shakespeare*. 3 vols. London, 1860.
Weber	H. Weber, ed. *The Works of Beaumont and Fletcher*. Vol. XIII. Edinburgh, 1812.

Introduction

PUBLICATION

The only quarto of *The Two Noble Kinsmen* was printed by Thomas Cotes for John Waterson in 1634. The title reads: "THE TWO NOBLE KINSMEN: Presented at the Blackfriers by the Kings Maiesties servants, with great applause: Written by the memorable Worthies of their time; [brace] Mr. *John Fletcher*, and Mr. *William Shakespeare* [brace] *Gent*." The play was entered to Waterson on the Stationers' Register on April 8 as "a TragiComedy called the two noble kinsmen, by Io: ffletcher and Wm. Shakespeare." The printed text includes stage directions naming actors which indicate that Waterson had obtained the manuscript from its original owners, the King's Men. On October 30, 1646, Waterson transferred his copyright in "The Noble kinsman, by Mr Flesher" to Humphrey Moseley. It was not included among the plays attributed to Shakespeare which were added as a supplement to the second issue of the third folio in 1664. P. Bertram explains this on the grounds that at that date the copyright still belonged to Moseley's widow, from whom it later passed to the publishers of the Beaumont and Fletcher folio of 1679, in which *The Two Noble Kinsmen* was printed without reference to Shakespeare as part-author.[1] It has since been reprinted in all collected editions of Beaumont and Fletcher. It was included in the "Doubtful Plays" volume of Charles Knight's *Pictorial Shakespeare* in 1841 and Alexander Dyce admitted it to the Shakespeare canon in his second edition of Shakespeare in 1866. A few later editors have followed suit. The standard edition, by Harold Littledale, published by the New Shakespeare Society, 1876–1885, is a storehouse of information about the play and provides the fullest account of verbal parallels between it and Shakespeare's canonical works.

[1] P. Bertram, *Shakespeare and "The Two Noble Kinsmen"* (New Brunswick, 1965), pp. 15–16.

DATE AND EARLY PERFORMANCES

The play was first acted by the King's Men at their private theater in the Blackfriars, probably during the winter of 1613–1614. The morris dancers in III.v are borrowed from the second anti-masque in Beaumont's *Masque of the Inner Temple and Gray's Inn*, which was presented at Whitehall before James I on February 20, 1613, during the festivities for the wedding of Princess Elizabeth to Frederick, Elector Palatine. This establishes the earliest likely date of performance as the late summer of 1613. The later limit is given by allusions in Ben Jonson's *Bartholomew Fair*, first performed on October 31, 1614. These include:

QUARLOUS.
. . . Well, my word is out of the *Arcadia*, then: "Argalus."
WINWIFE.
And mine out of the play, "Palemon."

(IV.iii.68–70)

and

QUARLOUS.
. . . Master Winwife, give you joy, you are Palemon, you are possess'd o' the gentlewoman . . . (V.vi.85–86).

A Revels Office note, usually dated about 1619, lists play titles including *The Two Noble Kinsmen*: this may point to a revival at Court in 1619 or 1620. The 1634 quarto prints two stage directions which name the actors of minor parts; see textual notes on IV.ii.70.1 and V.iii.0.1. The men in question, Curtis Greville and Thomas Tuckfield, were both with the King's Men only about 1625–1626. As the death of James I and the plague combined to keep the theaters shut from March to November, 1625, the revival in which Greville and Tuckfield appeared must have taken place soon after November, 1625. The prologue and epilogue belong to a revival, as the reference to the play's earlier loss of its "maidenhead" (Prologue, ll. 1–8), clearly indicates. If they belong to the revival of 1625–1626, "our losses" (Prologue, l. 32), could refer to the deaths of James I and of John Fletcher in 1625.

No later seventeenth-century performances are recorded. Sir William Davenant's adaptation of the play, *The Rivals*, was performed in 1664 and printed, anonymously, after his death in 1668.

AUTHORSHIP

By 1608 Shakespeare had been established for fourteen years as the leading dramatist of the King's Men. The performance of *Pericles* at about this date marked the beginning of the final stage of his career, in which he also wrote *Cymbeline* (1609–1610), *The Winter's Tale* (1610–1611), *The Tempest* (1611), as well as *Henry VIII* (1612–1613) and the lost play of *Cardenio* (performed in 1612), in which he is thought to have collaborated with John Fletcher. Although *Cymbeline*, *The Winter's Tale*, and *Henry VIII* were certainly performed at the company's public theater, the Globe, all these plays share features of style and stagecraft which suggest that Shakespeare wrote them to be equally suitable for the smaller stage and more sophisticated audience of the Blackfriars private theater, which his company acquired in 1608 and used from the winter of 1609–1610.[2]

The tradition that Shakespeare "in his elder days lived at Stratford" was recorded by John Ward in the early 1660's. He was evidently living in Stratford by June, 1611, because his cousin Thomas Greene had vacated New Place by that date, having earlier had his tenancy of it unexpectedly renewed for a year from September, 1609. But retirement no more caused Shakespeare to sever his connections with London than his dramatic career had led him to neglect Stratford affairs. He was in London in May, 1612, to testify in the case of Bellot v. Mountjoy, when he was described as "of Stratford upon Avon," and again in March, 1613, when he bought a house in the Blackfriars for £140. On this visit he may have been concerned with the rehearsals of *Henry VIII*, if the tradition that he trained John Lowin in the part of the king is true. His last recorded visit was in November 1614. He certainly kept in touch with his former colleagues and there is no intrinsic improbability involved in supposing that he made a brief return to writing in 1613, especially if the composition of *The Two Noble Kinsmen* was prompted by the emergency created by the Globe fire. Shakespeare revised his will on March 25, 1616, as a result of the marriage of his daughter Judith to Thomas Quiney in February. He was "in perfect health and memory" and his death, on April 23, at the end of his fifty-second year, need not be seen as the outcome of age, exhaustion, or prolonged disease.

[2] G. E. Bentley, "Shakespeare and the Blackfriars Theatre," *Shakespeare Survey*, I (1948), 38–50.

The career of Francis Beaumont (born about 1584) and John Fletcher (born 1579) as collaborative playwrights began between 1607 and 1609 and ended in 1613 or 1614, when Beaumont moved out of London after his marriage to Ursula Isley. Beaumont and Fletcher wrote twelve plays together, of which the most successful were two tragicomedies, *Philaster* (by 1610) and *A King and No King* (1611), one tragedy, *The Maid's Tragedy* (by 1611), and *The Scornful Lady* (1613), the last of their comedies. These plays quickly established them among the most highly reputed dramatists of the time, a position which Fletcher maintained after Beaumont's departure from London and subsequent death in March, 1616. In his later years, Fletcher collaborated most frequently with Philip Massinger (born 1583), who began to write plays for the King's Men soon after 1613 and who succeeded Fletcher as their principal dramatist after his death in the plague of 1625. In addition to his collaborations, Fletcher wrote many plays on his own throughout his career.

Fletcher's claim to the greater part of *The Two Noble Kinsmen* has rarely been questioned, but the identity of his collaborator or collaborators has been the subject of much controversy which has involved the names of Beaumont and Massinger as well as that of Shakespeare. Beaumont may have had a hand in the writing of the subplot, especially the scenes involving the morris dance (II.iv, III.v), but there are no grounds for supposing him to have been a major contributor and the whole question of his participation is complicated by uncertainty about the date of his marriage. If Massinger had anything to do with the text of the play as it was printed in 1634, which is far from certain, it may be that he overhauled the manuscript and wrote the prologue and epilogue for the revival of 1625–1626.[3] The claim that he was Fletcher's main collaborator, which enjoyed a brief vogue at the end of the nineteenth century, has been generally rejected.

Shakespeare's authorship of those parts of *The Two Noble Kinsmen* which are not evidently by Fletcher, though still disputed, is now as well established as it is ever likely to be. The complexity of the problem of attribution is such as to recommend caution in the

[3] Certain details of language, such as the unusual accentuation of "success" at I.i.209 and V.iii.69, are parallelled in his plays but not in those of Fletcher or Shakespeare.

statement of conclusions. The history of the controversy shows that many critics who have expressed strong views for or against Shakespeare have subsequently changed their minds. Reluctance to accept the play as Shakespeare's, even in part, often stems from the feeling that it is not a good enough play to have his name attached to it. This attitude is colored by the assumption that *The Tempest* is the crowning work of Shakespeare's genius and that it is inconceivable that he should subsequently have written more and have written it less well. The irrelevance of such considerations will be clear if we remember that the claim for Shakespeare's authorship is limited to no more than a third of the play and that, although there is reason to suppose that he may have planned the whole play in outline, it owes its final form to Fletcher.

Acceptance of Shakespeare as part-author of *The Two Noble Kinsmen* is urged by positive evidence, both external and internal, as well as by the lack of a feasible alternative attribution.

External evidence relating to the authorship of the play consists of two facts. It was excluded from the Shakespeare first folio in 1623 and it was attributed to Fletcher and Shakespeare in 1634, both in the Stationers' Register and on the quarto title page. Exclusion from the folio would argue strongly against Shakespeare's authorship if the whole play were in question, but in no play in the folio is his role that of minor collaborator. The exclusion of *Pericles*, in which he certainly had a hand, can be best accounted for on the grounds either that it is a collaborative play, or that Heminge and Condell had access to no better text than that of the 1609 quarto and thought it too corrupt to be included. The text of *The Two Noble Kinsmen* is a very good one. Heminge and Condell therefore excluded it either because they had no access to the manuscript in 1622–1623, or because they knew that Shakespeare had no hand in it, or because they knew it to be a collaborative play in which his was a minor share. Greater certainty is hardly possible, but at least we may conclude that their decision does not wholly rule out the possibility that Shakespeare had a hand in the play.

The attribution on the quarto title page has high authority, not because title pages tend in general to be accurate in assigning authorship, but because John Waterson published a number of other plays belonging to the King's Men with attributions that have not been questioned.[4] He evidently obtained the manuscript from the King's Men and they were better placed than anyone else to know who wrote the play.

In this situation internal evidence is of crucial importance both in attempting to answer the question of Shakespeare's share in the play and in reaching an estimate of the respective shares of the two authors.

Attentive readers of *The Two Noble Kinsmen* have always been aware that the play contains passages in two markedly different styles. When he adapted it in the 1660's, Davenant followed closely only the scenes which have since come to be regarded as Fletcher's, while "some of those scenes which have been most strongly held for Shakespeare were flung aside by his wilful godson, who found no use for the riches of the first and last acts."[5] The earliest description of these styles was written by Charles Lamb in answer to George Steevens, who claimed the whole play for Fletcher: "That Fletcher should have copied Shakespeare's manner through so many entire scenes (which is the theory of Mr. Steevens) is not very probable, that he could have done it with such facility is to me not certain. His ideas moved slow; his versification, though sweet, is tedious, it stops every moment; he lays line upon line, making up one after the other, adding image to image so deliberately that we see where they join: Shakespeare mingles every thing, he runs line into line, embarrasses sentences and metaphors; before one idea has burst its shell, another has hatched and is clamorous for disclosure. If Fletcher wrote some scenes in imitation, why did he stop? or shall we say that Shakespeare wrote the other scenes in imitation of Fletcher?"[6]

Attempts to prove the authorship on internal grounds have confirmed the presence of two styles in the play and have shown that they alternate more or less as follows:

A (Shakespeare): I; III.i, ii; V.i.iii–iv.
B (Fletcher): II.ii–vi; III.iii–vi; IV.i–ii; V.ii.

Doubt has most often been expressed about three verse scenes, I.v, III.ii, and IV.ii, and about the only two prose scenes, II.i and IV.iii,

[4] They include Webster's *The Duchess of Malfi* (1623) and Fletcher's *The Elder Brother* (1637) and *Monsieur Thomas* (1639).

[5] A. C. Sprague, *Beaumont and Fletcher on the Restoration Stage* (Cambridge, Mass., 1926), p. 129.

[6] C. Lamb, *Specimens of English Dramatic Poets* (London, 1808), p. 419.

which are often given to Shakespeare. Although this division is probably correct in outline, no certainty yet exists about the mode of collaboration and it is very likely that the Shakespeare scenes contain lines or even longer passages by Fletcher; e.g., V.i.1–33. Whatever the mode of collaboration, the final text, as we have it, would seem to have been overseen by Fletcher rather than Shakespeare. G. L. Kittredge was of the opinion that "exact details are beyond the scope of sane criticism."[7]

The most impressive tests are those which provide objective verification of the observed varieties of style. Metrical tests, although inaccurately applied in the nineteenth century, indicate substantial variation between the two main groups of verse scenes in the frequency of unstressed final monosyllables and of run-on lines.[8] A. Hart's examination of the vocabulary of the play shows striking differences between the two sections in the frequency of verbal coinages and unfamiliar compounded forms, and relates the vocabulary of section A to the linguistic usage of Shakespeare's latest plays.[9] A. C. Bradley pointed out a further correlation between the A scenes and Shakespeare's late plays, showing that verse scenes ending with a half-line are frequent in Shakespeare and very rare in Fletcher.[10]

Verbal parallels are notoriously two-edged as evidence of authorship: they may be merely commonplace or they may result from imitation, conscious or unconscious. *The Two Noble Kinsmen* is full of verbal parallels with the plays of Shakespeare. It is possible to suggest a distinction between parallels of more or less mechanical exactitude. The less mechanical class may be illustrated by comparing V.i.81–87,130, with these lines from *Cymbeline*,

> I had rather
> Have skipp'd from sixteen years of age to sixty:
> To have turn'd my leaping time into a crutch,
> Than have seen this.   (IV.ii.198–201)

[7] G. L. Kittredge, ed., *The Complete Works of Shakespeare* (Boston, 1936), p. 1409.

[8] *The Two Noble Kinsmen*, ed., H. Littledale (London, 1876, 1885), pp. 19*–23*; cf. A. Oras," 'Extra Monosyllables' in *Henry VIII* and the problem of Authorship," *Journal of English and Germanic Philology*, LII (1953), 198–213.

[9] A. Hart, "Shakespeare and the Vocabulary of *The Two Noble Kinsmen*," *The Review of English Studies*, X (1934), 274–287.

[10] A. C. Bradley, *A Miscellany* (London, 1929), pp. 218–224.

Similarity of expression here reflects similarity of context: both passages are concerned with the contrast between youth and age. The other class is exemplified in III.ii, a scene of very doubtful authorship, which echoes *Hamlet* at l. 20 and *Macbeth* at l. 35 in the phrases "How stand I then" and "The moon is down" (see explanatory notes). Parallels of the first class may be indicative of Shakespeare's authorship, those of the second are ambiguous, and may even be taken as evidence against it, as he was not given to such mechanical repetition of himself. Such echoes of Shakespeare are frequent in the plays of Beaumont, Fletcher, and Massinger, in whose early diet as playgoers his plays must have figured largely.

"Image-clusters," groups of associatively linked words habitually found together, have been identified in the plays of Shakespeare.[11] The presence of some of these clusters in *The Two Noble Kinsmen* has been urged as proof of Shakespeare's hand in the play, but the evidence is ambiguous as it has not been demonstrated that one poet's "image-clusters" can never become the imaginative property of another who knows his work.[12]

The evidence of poets' personal preferences for certain colloquial and contracted verbal forms has served to confirm Fletcher's share in the play, but is not effective as proof of Shakespeare's hand in it. The forms found in A are, however, at least consistent with the hypothesis that Shakespeare wrote the scenes in question.[13]

The internal evidence for dual authorship is not only stylistic. Too much has sometimes been made of inconsistencies in the characterization: we may smile at the indignation with which Littledale distinguished the Doctor in IV.iii, "so professional, so intelligent, so homogeneous with Shakespeare's other mad doctors," from "the despicable pander who goes by the name of 'Doctor' in V.ii."[14] This is mere prudery, not criticism, but inconsistencies do still exist, not important enough to disrupt the play in performance, but quite clearly resulting from differing aims and differing conceptions of the characters. The behavior of Palamon and Arcite in prison

[11] E. A. Armstrong, *Shakespeare's Imagination* (London, 1946).

[12] M. Mincoff, "The Authorship of *The Two Noble Kinsmen*," *English Studies*, XXXIII (1952), 97–115; K. Muir, "Shakespeare's Hand in *The Two Noble Kinsmen*," *Shakespeare Survey*, XI (1958), 50–59; E. A. Armstrong, *Shakespeare's Imagination*, 2nd edn. (Lincoln, Nebraska, 1963), Appendix B.

[13] C. Hoy, "The Shares of Fletcher and his Collaborators in the Beaumont and Fletcher Canon," *Studies in Bibliography*, XV (1962), 71–90.

[14] Littledale, *op. cit.*, p. 61*.

(II.ii) does not match the description of it given by the Jailer's Daughter at II.i.35–41, and Palamon's boast to Venus at V.i.98–107 shows a complete unawareness of what happened at III.iii.28–41. Inconsistencies of detail pass unnoticed in most of Shakespeare's plays, but these are inconsistencies of purpose: II.ii and III.iii are written for immediate effects of pathos and excitement, II.i and V.i are more concerned with a wider scheme of ideas and values. Minor inconsistencies indicative of dual authorship include the use of two forms of the name Pirithous. In Act I the name is trisyllabic, and is scanned "Pírithóus"; in Acts II and IV it has four syllables and the correct classical accentuation "Piríthoús."[15] The incorrect accentuation is generally associated in the quarto with the spellings "Pirithous, Pyrithous," the correct with the spelling "Perithous." This suggests that the two authors may have learned the name from different sources: the character is called Pirithous in North's Plutarch and Perithous in Chaucer's *Knight's Tale*.[16]

The aim of collaborating playwrights was to write a play, not to leave to posterity clear evidence of their respective shares in it. *The Two Noble Kinsmen* is a play which bears signs of its origin but it achieves a degree of coherence sufficient to have made it a success in its own day. The question of collaboration is of importance for twentieth-century readers because it affords an explanation for a common response to the play, that it begins and ends with a splendor of language that is not sustained in the middle acts but that those middle acts are much easier to follow and would probably have a much more immediate hold on an audience.[17]

SOURCES

The main plot is derived, as the Prologue tells us, from Chaucer. *The Knight's Tale* of Palamon and Arcite is the first of the *Canterbury Tales*. It is very freely adapted in Acts I and V but the other main-plot scenes which follow it do so faithfully and contain some verbal echoes of the tale. Act I also draws on Sir Thomas North's translation

---

15 I.i.207, 219, I.iii.55, 95; II.ii.247, II.v.31; IV.i.13.

16 T. Speght, ed., *The Works of Our Ancient and Learned English Poet Geoffrey Chaucer* (1602), folios 1–10.

17 D. V. Erdman and E. G. Fogel, *Evidence for Authorship* (Ithaca, N.Y., 1966), pp. 486–494, summarizes recent contributions to the authorship question.

of Plutarch's "Life of Theseus" for the relationship of Theseus to Pirithous and for his admiration of Hercules. North's description of the "turnings and crankes of the *Labyrinth*" is echoed at I.ii.28. Both books had earlier been used by Shakespeare for *A Midsummer Night's Dream*, whose action is framed by the wedding festivities of Theseus and Hippolyta. It is unclear whether the poets referred to other books bearing on their main plot. The care shown by Theseus for the wounded after the battle and the confusion of Emilia faced with the need to choose between the rival attractions of Palamon and Arcite are among features of the play which resemble Chaucer's source, Boccaccio's *Teseida*, more closely than *The Knight's Tale*, but these are changes of emphasis which could easily have occurred to the authors in the process of adapting Chaucer and do not demonstrate that they knew Boccaccio's poem or the prose versions of it which were printed in the sixteenth century in Italian and French. Similarly some classical texts relating to Thebes, such as the *Thebais* of Statius, were probably known to Shakespeare or Fletcher. Shakespeare knew how to spell the name Capaneus ("Campaneo" in Chaucer) though not how to scan it,[18] while Palamon's allusion to Juno's jealousy of Thebes, at I.ii.20–22, implies a fuller knowledge of the story of Thebes than Chaucer could supply.

Other sources have been identified for particular incidents in the play. The manner of Palamon's return to Athens (II.iii, v) recalls *Pericles*, II.ii and iii. The schoolmaster in III.v owes something, in general and in detail, to Rhombus in Sir Philip Sidney's entertainment "The Lady of May" and the episode in which he figures also recalls the entertainments in *Love's Labour's Lost*, V.ii, and *A Midsummer Night's Dream*: like Nick Bottom, the countrymen are weavers of Athens. The dancers described at III.v.121–129 correspond with eight of the twelve dancers in the second anti-masque in Beaumont's *Masque of the Inner Temple*, "consisting of May Lord, May Lady. Servingman, Chambermaide. A Countery Clowne, or Shepheard, Countrey Wench. An Host, Hostesse. A Hee Baboone, Shee Baboone. A Hee Foole, Shee Foole. a Pedant ushering them in."[19]

No direct source for the subplot concerning the Jailer's daughter has been identified and probably none exists. Her successive predicaments are the commonplaces of pastoral romance; if her madness

[18] I.i.59.

[19] F. T. Bowers, ed., *The Dramatic Works in the Beaumont and Fletcher Canon*, I (Cambridge, 1966), 133.

sometimes recalls Ophelia, her earlier solitary wanderings rather resemble those of Viola in Beaumont and Fletcher's *The Coxcomb* (1608–1610).

Two earlier plays of *Palamon and Arcite* have not survived. The first, by Richard Edwardes, was performed before Queen Elizabeth at Christ Church, Oxford, on September 2 and 4, 1566. Descriptions of it do not suggest any connection with our play.[20] The second was performed by the Admiral's men in the autumn of 1594.[21]

THE PLAY

The Two Noble Kinsmen belongs to the vogue of tragicomedy that began about 1609 with the revival of the old play of *Mucedorus* and with the writing of *Cymbeline* and *Philaster*. It differs from these plays in sustaining to the end a somber note which they dispel in the resolution of their plots. *The Knight's Tale* prescribed the death of Arcite, but the death sentence imposed on the losers in the tournament is not in Chaucer and the emphasis on mortality which pervades Act I is present only at the end of the tale.

Where Chaucer is concerned with the subtle workings of Fortune, the play lays its emphasis on the destructive power of love. "Is this winning?" cries Emilia, as she is awarded to Arcite and Palamon is led to execution. Palamon too, when he is reprieved and Arcite is dead, is conscious mainly of regret:

> O cousin,
> That we should things desire, which do cost us
> The loss of our desire! That nought could buy
> Dear love, but loss of dear love! (V.iv.109–112)

The theme of the bitterness of love is not illustrated only by the cousins' destructive rivalry. Palamon's prayer to Venus in V.i invokes her power in grotesque images which stress the need to placate a deity so inimical to rationality and human dignity. As C. Leech has pointed out, the same destructive power of Venus is exemplified in pathetic and comic terms in the "pretty" distemper of the Jailer's daughter.[22]

[20] E. K. Chambers, *The Elizabethan Stage*, I (Oxford, 1923), 128.

[21] R. A. Foakes and R. T. Rickert, eds., *Henslowe's Diary* (Cambridge, 1961), pp. 24, 25.

[22] C. Leech, ed., *The Two Noble Kinsmen* (New York, 1966), xxxii–xxxiii.

To offset the picture of irrational and destructive passion, Act I introduces, in the marriage of Theseus and Hippolyta, a love that asserts the natural order instead of disrupting it. Theseus has "shrunk" the Queen of the Amazons into "the bound she was o'erflowing" and Hippolyta, whose subjection to Theseus is voluntary, is ready to postpone her "joy" in order that Theseus may aid the three Queens before concluding the wedding ceremony. Sexual love is here shown under the control of reason, but another love is also exemplified which is not destructive because it is asexual. I.iii is largely devoted to the description of such love, between Theseus and Pirithous, and between Emilia and "the maid Flavina," who died in childhood innocence. The contrast between childish innocence and sexual experience recalls passages in Shakespeare's late plays; in *The Winter's Tale*, where Polixenes evokes his early friendship with Leontes, before sexual maturity taught them "the doctrine of ill-doing"; or in *Cymbeline*, where the jealous passion of Posthumus contrasts with the innocent fraternal love of Guiderius and Arviragus for Imogen in her disguise as Fidele.

P. Edwards gives a convincing account of the design of the play: "We are given, clearly enough, a life in two stages: youth, in which the passion of spontaneous friendship is dominant, and the riper age in which there is a dominant sexual passion, leading to marriage where it can. The movement from one stage to the next, the unavoidable process of growth, is a movement away from innocence, away from joy."[23] Edwards attributes this central idea to Shakespeare, but concedes that Fletcher's treatment of it in the middle acts is superficial and regrets that "Shakespeare did not write the whole of the play." In Acts I and V the main conflicts are thematic. They involve Mars, patron of the soldiers—Theseus, Pirithous, Palamon and Arcite—and upholder of military honor, and Venus, whose power over the senses and passions is inimical both to honor and to the chaste bonds of friendship. The climax of the thematic conflict is reached in V.i with the prayers of Arcite, Palamon, and Emilia to their divine patrons.

The strangest effect of collaborative authorship is that the central action involving Palamon and Arcite does not seem to bear any essential relation to this broader thematic conflict. Palamon is, indeed, presented as a lover and Arcite as a soldier (at III.vi.282–285)

---

[23] P. Edwards, "On the Design of *The Two Noble Kinsmen*," *A Review of English Literature*, V (1964), 103–104.

but the distinction is merely nominal. The reason for this is that one principle governing the writing of the later acts is that of suspense. The characterization of the kinsmen as "twins of honor" is designed to establish the conflict between them as one of personal merit and to keep its outcome uncertain for as long as possible. This end could be achieved only by minimizing differences between them and by leaving in the background their respective association with Venus and Mars. Even that small degree of moral superiority enjoyed by Palamon in Chaucer is suppressed as the cousins are not bound by an oath "Neither of us in love to hyndre oother,"[24] although the result is to reduce Palamon's outraged "I saw her first" to the level of the ridiculous. The uncertainty of the outcome is urged by Emilia's doubts in IV.ii and V.iii and by the description of the knights in IV.ii: Palamon's first knight is duly described as a lover, Arcite's as a soldier, but the third knight is described as a composite of lover and soldier and is assigned to neither party. Palamon is to be the winner, and in retrospect we can see this as the proper outcome, if only because the Jailer's daughter has weighted the scales in his favor; but the process of maintaining suspense led Fletcher to alienate sympathy from him in Act III, where his uncontrolled fury at Arcite's "falsehood" contrasts unpleasantly with Arcite's self-possession.

Chaucer's Emilie is vowed to virginity: so is Emilia in Act I and Act V, scene i, of the play. Elsewhere she is shown to be susceptible to the charms of both lovers. She is faced with two choices, between marriage and virginity and between Palamon and Arcite: both choices are made for her by the gods, but only after her perplexity has been presented at length. In the end, like Silvia in *The Two Gentlemen of Verona*, she is reduced to the status of a possession and is restored to Palamon by Arcite as "your stol'n jewel."

The impressiveness of *The Two Noble Kinsmen* lies not in its characters, who are not compelling either as psychological studies or as emblematic figures, but in its mastery of the tragicomic effects, pathos and suspense, and especially in its success, against the odds, in persuading us that its story, which teeters constantly on the verge of absurdity, is a fit vehicle for a poetic exploration of the inscrutability of the gods and of the dangerous power of love. The success is precarious and the tone of heroic hyperbole which makes it

---

[24] F. N. Robinson, ed., *The Works of Geoffrey Chaucer* (London, 1957), *The Knight's Tale*, l. 1135.

possible is sustained only at the cost of emotional involvement and of that range of ironic awareness which usually characterizes Shakespeare's earlier handling of similar themes.

The Two Noble Kinsmen is not best approached as a sequel to The Winter's Tale and The Tempest: Cymbeline and Philaster bear closer affinities to it both in theme and in tone. Its use of elaborate stage spectacle is one of its closest points of contact with Shakespeare's late plays. The Shakespeare scenes, as T. Spencer remarked, "are static and, though with splendor, stiff," expressing themselves in gesture and tableau rather than in action.[25] Their visual impact is often one of incongruous juxtaposition: the wedding procession is stopped by the mourning Queens in I.i; the bridegroom is summoned from the scaffold in V.iv. Such images must have had a peculiar power in the London of 1613, which had within the previous year seen the wedding festivities of its princess postponed for the funeral of the Prince of Wales.

THE TEXT

The quarto printed by Thomas Cotes in 1634 is the only authority for the text of The Two Noble Kinsmen. The text is a good one. It was printed from a promptbook, probably consisting of a scribal transcript of the text annotated by the book-keeper with extra stage directions, notes of properties needed, and the casting of some minor roles. The actors' names, "Curtis" at IV.ii.70.1 and V.iii.0.1 and "T. Tucke" at V.iii.0.1, must have been written in about 1625 and the marginal stage directions may have been added at the same time. They are printed in the outer margins in small roman type, not the italic used for the other directions, and occur at I.iii.58, I.iv.26; II.v.0.1; III.i.0.1, III.v.63, 132.1, III.vi.93. It has been suggested that they were in the hand of Edward Knight, book-keeper to the King's players in 1632 and 1633, but certainly associated with the company by 1624.[26]

The consistency of distribution of various spellings throughout the quarto suggests that it was set by a single compositor from a scribal manuscript. Fletcher's preference for the form *ye* over *you* is less noticeable than might be expected in the scenes attributed to him. As in other plays of Fletcher's where this occurs, the explanation

[25] T. Spencer, "The Two Noble Kinsmen," Modern Philology, XXXVI (1939), 257.

[26] W. W. Greg, The Shakespeare First Folio (Oxford, 1955), pp. 77–78, 100.

may be that the transcriber's own preference for *you* led him to alter many of Fletcher's *ye* forms.[27] The hypothesis that the manuscript was authorial has been put forward, with reservations, by F. O. Waller, who sees some "foul papers" characteristics in the quarto text.[28] These include the use of the name *Keeper* in the stage directions and speech prefixes of II.ii for the character who appears elsewhere as *Jailer* and the presence of textual cruces, especially the incomplete lines at V.i.50 and V.iv.77. P. Bertram is confident that the manuscript was a fair copy and in Shakespeare's hand throughout. As he also believes that Shakespeare was the author of the whole play, and as his evidence consists largely of spellings which are found outside Shakespeare's work, his position is doubtful, but he does succeed in challenging Waller's hypothesis of "foul papers."[29]

The two prose scenes, II.i and IV.iii, are printed as if they were verse, with capitals at the start of each line. The likeliest explanation is that the compositor, having cast off his copy by counting the lines, retained the lining of the manuscript even for prose and followed his usual verse-setting habit of beginning the lines with capitals because he was setting short lines and justifying them at the end as if they were verse. Correct prose-lining is found at IV.iii.35–49, at the foot of K2ᵛ. As it follows a passage of particularly short lines it looks like an attempt to compensate for wastage of space in the top half of the page. The verse-lining is resumed on K3. The two speeches correctly lined as prose follow an erroneous *Exit* for the Jailer's daughter, so that it is possible that this explanation is incorrect and that the compositor has reproduced a peculiarity of his copy.

Mislining of verse as prose also occurs. It affects extended passages in II.iii, III.iii, III.v, and V.ii. I have lined as verse all passages in verse scenes in which blank verse movement is perceptible. The occurrence of irregular verse lines elsewhere in the play seems to justify this procedure, even where it produces an occasional line which might not pass for verse out of context. My lining corresponds closely to that of Dyce. Bertram's contention that the mislined passages are really in prose is apparently based on the assumption that every verse line in a blank verse play must be both decasyllabic and iambic, an assumption not shared by Fletcher.

27 C. Hoy, "The Shares of Fletcher and his Collaborators in the Beaumont and Fletcher Canon," *Studies in Bibliography*, XI (1958), 85–86.

28 F. O. Waller, "The Printer's Copy for *The Two Noble Kinsmen*," *Studies in Bibliography*, XI (1958), 61–84.

29 Bertram, *op. cit.*, Chapter II.

Three scenes are misnumbered in the quarto: II.v is headed "Scaena 4"; III.v and vi are headed "Scaena 6" and "Scaena 7." These errors may reflect some initial doubt about the sequence of scenes, especially of the four soliloquies of the Jailer's daughter which constitute II.iv and vi, III.ii and iv. As these scenes have little bearing on the main plot, their placing is controlled mainly by the need to separate them from each other. If they were rearranged, making II.iv into II.vi, and calling II.vi, III.i, the misnumbered scenes would be correctly numbered, although III.i to iv would cease to be so.

II.i and II.ii are effectively a single scene. I. Smith has proposed that Palamon and Arcite should play them both from two adjacent windows belonging to an upper stage.[30] I note the quarto scene division and retain separate line numbering for II.ii both for ease of reference to earlier editions and because the scene division may mark a change of authorship.

Twelve copies of the quarto have been collated for this edition: seven in the Folger Shakespeare Library, two in the British Museum (C.34.g.23; C.117.b.51), the Dyce and Forster copies in the library of the Victoria and Albert Museum, and a microfilm of the copy in the University of Texas Library. Variants resulting from correction at press occur in the inner forme of sheets C and M and in the outer forme of sheets E and K: they are listed in the textual notes.

The unusually complex sentence-structure of the Shakespeare scenes has led me to punctuate in places with less regard for modern usage than for clarity of meaning.

I must express my thanks to the staffs of the Folger Shakespeare Library, the North Library of the British Museum and the library of the Victoria and Albert Museum for their help and courtesy and also my gratitude to the Director of the Folger Library and to the Humanities Research Committee of the University of Toronto for grants which enabled me to spend a summer at the Folger Library. The Delegates of the Clarendon Press, Oxford, have kindly permitted me to use for this edition some material collected for the critical old-spelling edition of the Shakespeare *Apocrypha* which I am preparing for them.

G. R. PROUDFOOT

King's College, London

[30] I. Smith, *Shakespeare's Blackfriars Playhouse* (London, 1966), pp. 377–378.

THE TWO NOBLE KINSMEN

[CHARACTERS OF THE PLAY

THESEUS, *Duke of Athens*
PIRITHOUS, *his friend*
PALAMON⎫
ARCITE ⎬ *the two noble kinsmen, nephews to Creon, King of Thebes*
JAILER
WOOER *of jailer's daughter*
GERROLD, *a schoolmaster*
DOCTOR
HIPPOLYTA, *Queen of the Amazons*
EMILIA, *her sister*
THREE QUEENS
JAILER'S DAUGHTER
HYMEN, *god of marriage*
BOY
ARTESIUS
VALERIUS
HERALD
WOMAN *attending Emilia*
FIVE COUNTRYMEN
FIVE WENCHES
TABORER
TWO FRIENDS *of Jailer*
JAILER'S BROTHER
GENTLEMAN
MESSENGER
SERVANT
SIX KNIGHTS
NYMPHS, ATTENDANTS, MAIDS, EXECUTIONER, GUARD]

PROLOGUE

Flourish.

New plays and maidenheads are near akin,
Much follow'd both, for both much money gi'en,
If they stand sound and well: and a good play—
Whose modest scenes blush on his marriage day
And shake to lose his honor—is like her   5
That after holy tie and first night's stir
Yet still is modesty, and still retains
More of the maid to sight, than husband's pains.
We pray our play may be so; for I am sure
It has a noble breeder and a pure,   10
A learned, and a poet never went
More famous yet 'twixt Po and silver Trent.
Chaucer, of all admir'd, the story gives,
There constant to eternity it lives;
If we let fall the nobleness of this,   15
And the first sound this child hear be a hiss,
How will it shake the bones of that good man
And make him cry from under ground, "O fan
From me the witless chaff of such a writer
That blasts my bays and my fam'd works makes lighter   20
Than Robin Hood!" This is the fear we bring;
For, to say truth, it were an endless thing
And too ambitious, to aspire to him,
Weak as we are, and almost breathless swim
In this deep water. Do but you hold out   25
Your helping hands, and we shall tack about

26. tack] *F;* take *Q.*

0.1. *Flourish*] fanfare, often to announce the approach of an important person.
   5. *honor*] virginity.
   6. *holy tie*] wedding.
   10. *breeder*] parent, i.e., source.
   15. *let fall*] fail to sustain.
   20. *blasts my bays*] destroys my poetical reputation.
   21. *Robin Hood*] a typical hero of popular ballads.
   25–26. *hold . . . hands*] applaud.
   26. *tack about*] turn a ship in the wind; the wind is here imagined as being produced by applause.

–4–

And something do to save us: you shall hear
Scenes, though below his art, may yet appear
Worth two hours' travel. To his bones sweet sleep:
Content to you. If this play do not keep   30
A little dull time from us, we perceive
Our losses fall so thick, we must needs leave.   *Flourish.*

---

29. *travel*] (1) journey; (2) labor.
31. *dull time*] period of slack trade.
32. *Our losses*] see Introduction, p. xii.

The Two Noble Kinsmen

Enter Hymen with a torch burning; a boy in a white robe before, singing and strewing flowers. After Hymen a nymph, encompass'd in her tresses, bearing a wheaten garland. Then Theseus, *between two other nymphs with wheaten chaplets on their heads. Then* Hippolyta, *the bride, led by* Pirithous, *and another holding a garland over her head, her tresses likewise hanging. After her,* Emilia, *holding up her train.* [Artesius and attendants.] *Music.*

THE SONG

Roses, their sharp spines being gone,
Not royal in their smells alone,
But in their hue;
Maiden pinks, of odor faint,
Daisies smell-less, yet most quaint,   5
And sweet thyme true;

Primrose, firstborn child of Ver,
Merry springtime's harbinger,
With her bells dim;
Oxlips, in their cradles growing,   10
Marigolds, on deathbeds blowing,
Lark's-heels trim;

0.4. Pirithous] *1750;* Theseus Q.   0.6. *Music*] Q *prints after* The Song.

0.1. *Hymen*] "The god of marriage, represented as a young man carrying a torch and veil" (*OED*).

0.3. *wheaten garland*] signifying fertility, but also virginity; cf. ll. 64–65; V.i.160.

0.4. *chaplets*] garlands.

5. *quaint*] pretty.

7. *Ver*] spring.

8. *harbinger*] herald.

12. *Lark's-heels*] larkspur.

All dear Nature's children sweet,
Lie 'fore bride and bridegroom's feet,
Blessing their sense.   *Strew flowers.*   15
Not an angel of the air,
Bird melodious, or bird fair,
Is absent hence.

The crow, the sland'rous cuckoo, nor
The boding raven, nor chough hoar,   20
Nor chatt'ring pie,
May on our bridehouse perch or sing,
Or with them any discord bring,
But from it fly.

Enter three Queens, *in black, with veils stained, with imperial crowns.*
The first Queen *falls down at the foot of* Theseus; *the second falls down at*
the foot of Hippolyta; *the third before* Emilia.

FIRST QUEEN.
        For pity's sake and true gentility's,   25
        Hear and respect me.
SECOND QUEEN.   For your mother's sake,
        And as you wish your womb may thrive with fair ones,
        Hear and respect me.
THIRD QUEEN.
        Now for the love of him whom Jove hath mark'd
        The honor of your bed, and for the sake   30
        Of clear virginity, be advocate
        For us and our distresses. This good deed
        Shall raze you out o'th' book of trespasses

16. *angel*] *F; angle Q.*   20. *chough hoar*] *1750; Clough hee Q.*

---

16. *angel*] bird of good omen.
19. *sland'rous*] mocking married men with its cry.
20. *boding*] prophetic of evil; Tilley, R 33.
20. *chough hoar*] gray-headed jackdaw.
21. *pie*] magpie.
24.1. *stained*] dyed.
26. *respect*] attend to.
29. *mark'd*] destined to be.
31. *clear*] pure.
33. *raze*] erase.
33. *book of trespasses*] record of sins.

All you are set down there.

THESEUS.

Sad lady, rise.

HIPPOLYTA.   Stand up.

EMILIA.   No knees to me.   35
What woman I may stead that is distress'd
Does bind me to her.

THESEUS.

What's your request? Deliver you for all.

FIRST QUEEN.

We are three queens whose sovereigns fell before
The wrath of cruel Creon; who endured   40
The beaks of ravens, talons of the kites
And pecks of crows in the foul fields of Thebes.
He will not suffer us to burn their bones,
To urn their ashes, nor to take th'offense
Of mortal loathsomeness from the blest eye   45
Of holy Phoebus, but infects the winds
With stench of our slain lords. O pity, duke!
Thou purger of the earth, draw thy fear'd sword
That does good turns to th' world; give us the bones
Of our dead kings, that we may chapel them;   50
And, of thy boundless goodness, take some note
That for our crowned heads we have no roof,
Save this, which is the lion's and the bear's,
And vault to every thing.

THESEUS.   Pray you, kneel not:
I was transported with your speech and suffer'd   55
Your knees to wrong themselves. I have heard the fortunes
Of your dead lords, which gives me such lamenting
As wakes my vengeance and revenge for 'em.

---

38. *Deliver*] speak.
40. *Creon*] King of Thebes after the deaths of Eteocles and Polynices,
sons of Oedipus.
46. *Phoebus*] Apollo, as god of the sun.
48. *Thou . . . earth*] The fame of Theseus was based on his killing of
monsters and robbers that infested Attica.
50. *chapel*] "To put (bury, etc.) in a chapel" (*OED*, only here).
54. *vault*] roof.

King Capaneus was your lord: the day
That he should marry you, at such a season   60
As now it is with me, I met your groom
By Mars's altar; you were that time fair,
Not Juno's mantle fairer than your tresses,
Nor in more bounty spread her; your wheaten wreath
Was then nor thresh'd nor blasted; fortune at you   65
Dimpled her cheek with smiles; Hercules our kinsman—
Then weaker than your eyes—laid by his club;
He tumbled down upon his Nemean hide
And swore his sinews thaw'd. O grief and time,
Fearful consumers, you will all devour.   70

FIRST QUEEN [*kneels*].
    O, I hope some god,
    Some god hath put his mercy in your manhood,
    Whereto he'll infuse power and press you forth
    Our undertaker.

THESEUS.   O no knees, none, widow:
    Unto the helmeted Bellona use them   75
    And pray for me, your soldier.
    Troubled I am.   *Turns away.*

SECOND QUEEN.   Honored Hippolyta,
    Most dreaded Amazonian, that hast slain
    The scythe-tusk'd boar; that with thy arm, as strong

---

59. lord:] *1711; no punct. in Q*.   68. Nemean] *1750;* Nenuan *Q*.

---

59. *Capaneus*] killed by a thunderbolt while attacking Thebes in the
army of Polynices; properly trisyllabic (Capáneus), but here with four
syllables (Cápanéus).
    60. *should*] was about to.
    61. *groom*] bridegroom.
    63. *Juno's mantle*] worn for her wedding with Jupiter; *Iliad*, xiv.
    68. *Nemean hide*] skin of the Nemean lion, killed by Hercules, who used
it as a cloak.
    73. *press*] force.
    74. *undertaker*] helper.
    75. *Bellona*] goddess of war.
    78. *Amazonian*] Hippolyta was queen of the Amazons.
    78–79. *that . . . boar*] perhaps an erroneous reference to the Calydonian
boar, whose hunters included Theseus and Pirithous, but not Hippolyta;
cf. III.v.17.

As it is white, wast near to make the male   80
To thy sex captive, but that this thy lord—
Born to uphold creation in that honor
First nature styl'd it in—shrunk thee into
The bound thou wast o'er-flowing, at once subduing
Thy force and thy affection: soldieress,   85
That equally canst poise sternness with pity,
Whom now I know hast much more power on him
Than ever he had on thee, who ow'st his strength
And his love too, who is a servant for
The tenor of thy speech: dear glass of ladies,   90
Bid him that we, whom flaming war doth scorch,
Under the shadow of his sword may cool us;
Require him he advance it o'er our heads;
Speak't in a woman's key, like such a woman
As any of us three; weep ere you fail.   95
Lend us a knee;
But touch the ground for us no longer time
Than a dove's motion when the head's pluck'd off;
Tell him, if he i'th' blood-siz'd field lay swoll'n,
Showing the sun his teeth, grinning at the moon,   100
What you would do.
HIPPOLYTA.   Poor lady, say no more:
I had as lief trace this good action with you
As that whereto I am going, and never yet
Went I so willing way. My lord is taken
Heart-deep with your distress: let him consider.   105

90. thy] *1750;* the *Q.*   104. willing way] *1750;* willing,
95–96.] *one line in Q.*   way *Q.*

80–85.] For Shakespeare's acceptance of the idea of male superiority,
see *Comedy of Errors*, II.i.16–25.
    83. *styl'd it in*] invested it with; created it for.
    84. *bound*] limit.
    86. *poise*] weigh.
    88. *ow'st*] ownest.
    89–90. *who is . . . speech*] who will do what you tell him; *tenor* = meaning.
    90. *glass of*] model for.
    94. *key*] tone of voice.
    99. *blood-siz'd*] smeared with blood.
    102. *lief*] gladly.
    102. *trace*] pass through, perform.

I'll speak anon.

THIRD QUEEN (*kneel to* Emilia). O, my petition was
　　Set down in ice, which by hot grief uncandied
　　Melts into drops; so sorrow, wanting form,
　　Is press'd with deeper matter.

EMILIA.　　　　　　　　　　　Pray stand up,
　　Your grief is written in your cheek.

THIRD QUEEN.　　　　　　　　O woe,　　　　　110
　　You cannot read it there; there, through my tears,
　　Like wrinkled pebbles in a glassy stream,
　　You may behold 'em. Lady, lady, alack,
　　He that will all the treasure know o'th' earth
　　Must know the center too; he that will fish　　115
　　For my least minnow, let him lead his line
　　To catch one at my heart. O pardon me,
　　Extremity, that sharpens sundry wits,
　　Makes me a fool.

EMILIA.　　　　　Pray you say nothing, pray you:
　　Who cannot feel nor see the rain, being in't,　　120
　　Knows neither wet nor dry. If that you were
　　The ground-piece of some painter, I would buy you
　　T'instruct me 'gainst a capital grief, indeed
　　Such heart-pierc'd demonstration; but alas,

---

106. S.D.] *Q prints after* was.　　　113. 'em.] *Weber; no punct. in Q.*
112. pebbles] *F;* peobles *Q.*　　　123. grief,] *this edn.; no punct. in Q.*
112. glassy] *1750;* glasse *Q.*

---

　106. *anon*] shortly.
　107. *uncandied*] thawed.
　108–109. *so . . . matter*] "so sorrow, lacking shape (i.e., power of expression), is oppressed with still greater occasion for it" (Skeat); or *press'd
with* could mean "forced into shape by," i.e., forced to express itself.
　111. *there; there*] The first *there* refers to her cheek, the second to her eyes.
　114–115. *He . . . too*] treasure is not to be acquired without digging for it.
　115. *center*] center of the earth.
　116. *lead*] weight with a lead sinker.
　118. *Extremity*] extreme suffering.
　122. *ground-piece*] "dull, lifeless, pictured-surface" (Littledale); the word
is not recorded elsewhere. The context demands a sense in strong contrast
to "a natural sister of our sex" in l. 125.
　123. *capital*] deadly.
　124. *Such . . . demonstration*] such an expression of a pierced heart as
yours is.

Being a natural sister of our sex,   125
Your sorrow beats so ardently upon me,
That it shall make a counter-reflect 'gainst
My brother's heart and warm it to some pity,
Though it were made of stone: pray have good comfort.

THESEUS.
Forward to th' temple; leave not out a jot   130
O'th' sacred ceremony.

FIRST QUEEN.   O, this celebration
Will longer last and be more costly than
Your suppliants' war! Remember that your fame
Knolls in the ear o'th world: what you do quickly
Is not done rashly; your first thought is more   135
Than others' labored meditance; your premeditating,
More than their actions: but, O Jove, your actions,
Soon as they moves, as ospreys do the fish,
Subdue before they touch. Think, dear duke, think
What beds our slain kings have.

SECOND QUEEN.   What griefs our beds,   140
That our dear lords have none.

THIRD QUEEN.   None fit for th' dead.
Those that with cords, knives, drams, precipitance,
Weary of this world's light, have to themselves
Been death's most horrid agents, human grace
Affords them dust and shadow.

FIRST QUEEN.   But our lords   145
Lie blist'ring 'fore the visitating sun,
And were good kings, when living.

THESEUS.   It is true,
And I will give you comfort,

132. longer] *1750;* long *Q.*   147–151.] *Q   lines   end: living/*
142. drams,] *1750; no punct, in Q.*   comfort/graves/Creon/doing.

---

125. *Being*] since you are.
127. *make a counter-reflect*] reflect back.
134. *Knolls*] sounds, rings.
136. *labored meditance*] careful thought.
138. *as ospreys . . . fish*] alluding to the belief that fish turned their bellies up to be caught as the osprey flew over them; cf. *Coriolanus,* IV.vii. 33–35.
142. *drams*] poisons.
142. *precipitance*] headlong fall.
146. *visitating*] scrutinizing (only here).

To give your dead lords graves: the which to do
Must make some work with Creon.
FIRST QUEEN.   And that work   150
Presents itself to th' doing:
Now 'twill take form, the heats are gone tomorrow.
Then, bootless toil must recompense itself
With its own sweat; now, he's secure,
Not dreams we stand before your puissance,   155
Rinsing our holy begging in our eyes
To make petition clear.
SECOND QUEEN.   Now you may take him,
Drunk with his victory.
THIRD QUEEN.   And his army full
Of bread and sloth.
THESEUS.   Artesius, that best knowest
How to draw out fit to this enterprise   160
The prim'st for this proceeding and the number
To carry such a business, forth and levy
Our worthiest instruments; whilst we dispatch
This grand act of our life, this daring deed
Of fate in wedlock.
FIRST QUEEN.   Dowagers, take hands;   165
Let us be widows to our woes; delay
Commends us to a famishing hope.
ALL QUEENS.   Farewell.

---

156. Rinsing] *1750;* Wrinching *Q.*   165. hands;] *1711; no punct. in Q.*
159. Artesius] *1750; Artesuis Q.*   167. S.P.] *All. Q.*

149. *To give*] by giving.
152. *heats*] enthusiasm.
153. *bootless*] unavailing.
154. *secure*] free from alarm.
157. *clear*] clean.
160. *draw out*] march soldiers out of camp.
160. *fit to*] either "prepare for" (with *fit* as verb) or "suitable for" (with *fit* as adjective).
161. *prim'st*] best.
162. *carry*] perform.
165. *Dowagers*] widows.
166. *Let . . . woes*] let us lament the death of our complaints (dead because Theseus is neglecting them).

SECOND QUEEN.
    We come unseasonably; but when could grief
    Cull forth, as unpanged judgment can, fitt'st time
    For best solicitation?
THESEUS.   Why, good ladies,   170
    This is a service, whereto I am going,
    Greater than any war; it more imports me
    Than all the actions that I have foregone
    Or futurely can cope.
FIRST QUEEN.   The more proclaiming
    Our suit shall be neglected, when her arms,   175
    Able to lock Jove from a synod, shall
    By warranting moonlight corslet thee; O when
    Her twinning cherries shall their sweetness fall
    Upon thy tasteful lips, what wilt thou think
    Of rotten kings or blubber'd queens? What care   180
    For what thou feel'st not? what thou feel'st being able
    To make Mars spurn his drum. O, if thou couch
    But one night with her, every hour in't will
    Take hostage of thee for a hundred, and
    Thou shalt remember nothing more than what   185
    That banquet bids thee to.
HIPPOLYTA.   Though much unlike
    You should be so transported, as much sorry
    I should be such a suitor, yet I think
    Did I not by th'abstaining of my joy,
    Which breeds a deeper longing, cure their surfeit,   190
    That craves a present med'cine, I should pluck

172. war] *1750;* was *Q.*   178. twinning] *1750;* twyning *Q.*

---

169. *Cull forth*] choose.
169. *unpanged judgment*] reason unaffected by pain.
175. *shall*] is bound to be.
176. *synod*] council.
177. *warranting*] sanctioning.
178. *twinning*] joining.
179. *tasteful*] able to taste.   182. *couch*] lie.
186–188. *Though . . . suitor*] Although it is as extremely improbable that you should be so carried away by passion as I would be sorry to beg you to be so.
190. *surfeit*] sickness resulting from excess (of grief).
191. *present*] immediate.

All ladies' scandal on me. [*Kneels.*]   Therefore, sir,
As I shall here make trial of my prayers,
Either presuming them to have some force,
Or sentencing for ay their vigor dumb,   195
Prorogue this business we are going about, and hang
Your shield afore your heart, about that neck
Which is my fee, and which I freely lend
To do these poor queens service.

ALL QUEENS.   O help now!
Our cause cries for your knee.

EMILIA [*kneels*].   If you grant not   200
My sister her petition, in that force,
With that celerity and nature, which
She makes it in, from henceforth I'll not dare
To ask you anything, nor be so hardy
Ever to take a husband.

THESEUS.   Pray stand up.   205
I am entreating of myself to do
That which you kneel to have me. —Pirithous,
Lead on the bride: get you and pray the gods
For success and return; omit not anything
In the pretended celebration. —Queens,   210
Follow your soldier.   [*To Artesius*].   —As before, hence you
And at the banks of Aulis meet us with
The forces you can raise, where we shall find
The moiety of a number for a business

212. Aulis] *1750;* Anly *Q.*

---

195. *ay*] ever.
196. *Prorogue*] postpone.
198. *fee*] property.
202. *With . . . nature*] as quickly and in the same spirit.
207. *Pirithous*] properly with four syllables (Pírithoús); here trisyllabic (Pírithoús); see Introduction, p. xix.
209. *success*] accented on the first syllable; cf. V.iii.69.
210. *pretended*] intended.
211. *your soldier*] Theseus himself.
212. *banks of Aulis*] Theobald's emendation has been generally accepted; Q's "Anly" does not exist. Although Aulis does not lie between Athens and Thebes, it is proposed as a meeting place because an Athenian force is there already.
214. *moiety*] half.

More bigger look'd.   [*Exit Artesius.*]
          —Since that our theme is haste,   215
I stamp this kiss upon thy current lip;
Sweet, keep it as my token. —Set you forward,
For I will see you gone.
Farewell, my beauteous sister. —Pirithous,
Keep the feast full; bate not an hour on't.

PIRITHOUS.   Sir,   220
I'll follow you at heels: the feast's solemnity
Shall want till your return.

THESEUS.   Cousin, I charge you,
Budge not from Athens. We shall be returning
Ere you can end this feast, of which, I pray you,
Make no abatement. Once more, farewell all.   225

   Exeunt [Hippolyta, Emilia, Pirithous *and train*] *towards the temple.*

FIRST QUEEN.
Thus dost thou still make good the tongue o'th' world.

SECOND QUEEN.
And earn'st a deity equal with Mars.

THIRD QUEEN.
If not above him, for
Thou being but mortal makest affections bend
To godlike honors; they themselves, some say,   230
Groan under such a mast'ry.

THESEUS.   As we are men,
Thus should we do; being sensually subdued,
We lose our human title. Good cheer, ladies!
Now turn we towards your comforts.   *Flourish. Exeunt.*

225.1.] *Q prints after l. 218.*

---

   215. *theme*] business.
   216. *current*] (1) running; (2) genuine (with reference to the metaphor of coining in *stamp* and *token*).
   217. *token*] keepsake.
   220. *bate*] omit.
   221. *solemnity*] dignity.
   222. *want*] be lacking.
   230–231. *they . . . mast'ry*] even the gods are said to be subject to such affections; *mast'ry* = rule; power.
   232. *sensually subdued*] subdued by the senses.

[I.ii]   *Enter* Palamon *and* Arcite.

ARCITE.

    Dear Palamon, dearer in love than blood
    And our prime cousin, yet unharden'd in
    The crimes of nature, let us leave the city
    Thebes, and the temptings in't, before we further
    Sully our gloss of youth.   5
    And here to keep in abstinence we shame
    As in incontinence; for not to swim
    I'th' aid o'th' current, were almost to sink,
    At least to frustrate striving; and to follow
    The common stream, 'twould bring us to an eddy   10
    Where we should turn or drown; if labor through,
    Our gain but life and weakness.
PALAMON.   Your advice
    Is cried up with example. What strange ruins,
    Since first we went to school, may we perceive
    Walking in Thebes? Scars and bare weeds   15
    The gain o'th' martialist, who did propound
    To his bold ends, honor and golden ingots,
    Which though he won, he had not; and now flirted
    By peace for whom he fought. Who then shall offer
    To Mars's so scorn'd altar? I do bleed   20
    When such I meet, and wish great Juno would
    Resume her ancient fit of jealousy

---

  2. *prime*] chief.
  5. *Sully*] defile.
  6. *keep*] remain; refering both to *here* and *in abstinence*.
  8. *I'th'* . . . *current*] with the current; "to swim with the stream," Tilley,
S 930.
  9. *to frustrate striving*] to try in vain.
  13. *cried up with*] recommended by.
  15. *bare weeds*] (1) threadbare clothes; (2) mere clothes.
  16. *martialist*] soldier.
  16. *propound*] propose as a reward.
  18. *flirted*] sneered at.
  21–22. *wish . . . jealousy*] Juno's inveterate hatred of Thebes arose as a
result of Jupiter's partiality for Theban women. The motif of Juno's
jealousy figures largely in Statius' *Thebais* and in Boccaccio's *Teseida* but
not in Chaucer's *Knight's Tale*.

To get the soldier work, that peace might purge
For her repletion and retain anew
Her charitable heart, now hard and harsher   25
Than strife or war could be.

ARCITE.   Are you not out?
Meet you no ruin but the soldier in
The cranks and turns of Thebes? You did begin
As if you met decays of many kinds.
Perceive you none that do arouse your pity   30
But th'unconsider'd soldier?

PALAMON.   Yes, I pity
Decays where'er I find them, but such most
That, sweating in an honorable toil,
Are paid with ice to cool 'em.

ARCITE.   'Tis not this
I did begin to speak of; this is virtue,   35
Of no respect in Thebes. I spake of Thebes,
How dangerous, if we will keep our honors,
It is for our residing; where every evil
Hath a good color; where ev'ry seeming good's
A certain evil; where not to be ev'n jump   40
As they are, here were to be strangers, and
Such things to be, mere monsters.

PALAMON.   'Tis in our power
(Unless we fear that apes can tutor's) to
Be masters of our manners. What need I
Affect another's gait, which is not catching   45
Where there is faith? Or to be fond upon

42. be,] *Littledale; no punct. in Q.*

23–24.] cf. V.i.64–66.
24. *repletion*] excess of eating or drinking.
24. *retain*] employ.
26. *out*] forgetting.
28. *cranks*] winding paths; see Introduction, p. xx.
39. *color*] appearance.
40–42. *where . . . monsters*] where failure to conform would make us strangers at home and conformity would make us no better than monsters.
40. *jump*] precisely.
43. *tutor's*] tutor us.
45. *gait*] manner of walking.
45. *catching*] (1) attractive; (2) infectious.
46. *faith*] self-reliance.

Another's way of speech, when by mine own
I may be reasonably conceiv'd, sav'd too,
Speaking it truly? Why am I bound
By any generous bond to follow him   50
Follows his tailor, haply so long until
The follow'd make pursuit? Or let me know
Why mine own barber is unblest, with him
My poor chin too, for 'tis not scissor'd just
To such a favorite's glass? What canon is there   55
That does command my rapier from my hip
To dangle't in my hand, or to go tip-toe
Before the street be foul? Either I am
The fore-horse in the team, or I am none
That draw i'th' sequent trace. These poor slight sores   60
Need not a plantain; that which rips my bosom
Almost to th' heart's—

ARCITE.   Our uncle Creon.

PALAMON.   He,
A most unbounded tyrant, whose successes
Makes heaven unfear'd and villainy assured
Beyond its power there's nothing; almost puts   65
Faith in a fever, and deifies alone
Voluble chance; who only attributes
The faculties of other instruments
To his own nerves and act; commands men service,
And what they win in't, boot and glory; one   70

---

65. power there's nothing;] *1750;*   70. glory; one] *Littledale;* glory on;
power: there's nothing, *Q.*   *Q (corr.); no punct. in Q (uncorr.).*

---

48. *conceiv'd*] understood.
49–50. *Why . . . bond*] what truly honorable obligation am I under?
50. *follow*] imitate.
51. *Follows*] follows the advice of.
52. *pursuit*] (1) chase; (2) lawsuit.
54. *for*] because.
55. *To . . . glass*] to imitate some favorite.
55. *canon*] law.
60. *draw . . . trace*] pull in the line (of horses) that follow.
63. *unbounded*] uncontrolled.
66. *Faith*] religious belief.
66. *alone*] only.
67. *Voluble chance*] inconstant fortune.
70. *boot*] profit.

That fears not to do harm; good, dares not. Let
The blood of mine that's sib to him be suck'd
From me with leeches. Let them break and fall
Off me with that corruption!

ARCITE.   Clear-spirited cousin,
Let's leave his court, that we may nothing share   75
Of his loud infamy: for our milk
Will relish of the pasture, and we must
Be vile, or disobedient; not his kinsmen
In blood, unless in quality.

PALAMON.   Nothing truer.
I think the echoes of his shames have deaf'd   80
The ears of heav'nly justice. Widow's cries
Descend again into their throats and have not
Due audience of the gods.

                    Enter Valerius.

                    Valerius.

VALERIUS.
The king calls for you; yet be leaden-footed
Till his great rage be off him. Phoebus, when   85
He broke his whipstock and exclaim'd against
The horses of the sun, but whisper'd to
The loudness of his fury.

PALAMON.   Small winds shake him.
But what's the matter?

VALERIUS.
Theseus, who where he threats appalls, hath sent   90
Deadly defiance to him and pronounces
Ruin to Thebes, who is at hand to seal
The promise of his wrath.

ARCITE.   Let him approach;
But that we fear the gods in him, he brings not

83. S.D.] *Q prints after l. 82.*

---

72. *sib*] related.

77. *relish*] taste.

85–87. *Phoebus . . . sun*] "The allusion is probably to the story of Phaëton
in Ovid; the day after Phaëton's death, Phoebus could hardly be persuaded
to drive the chariot of the sun once more, and wreaked some of his anger
upon the horses, which he lashed severely" (Skeat); Ovid *Metamorphoses*
ii. 397–399.

A jot of terror to us. Yet what man   95
Thirds his own worth—the case is each of ours—
When that his action's dregg'd with mind assur'd
'Tis bad he goes about.
PALAMON.   Leave that unreason'd.
Our services stand now for Thebes, not Creon:
Yet to be neutral to him were dishonor,   100
Rebellious to oppose; therefore we must
With him stand to the mercy of our fate,
Who hath bounded our last minute.
ARCITE.   So we must.—
Is't said this war's afoot, or it shall be
On fail of some condition?
VALERIUS.   'Tis in motion;   105
The intelligence of state came in the instant
With the defier.
PALAMON.   Let's to the king, who, were he
A quarter carrier of that honor which
His enemy come in, the blood we venture
Should be as for our health, which were not spent,   110
Rather laid out for purchase. But alas,
Our hands advanc'd before our hearts, what will
The fall o'th' stroke do damage?
ARCITE.   Let th'event,
That never-erring arbitrator, tell us,
When we know all ourselves, and let us follow   115
The becking of our chance.   *Exeunt.*

[I.iii]   *Enter* Pirithous, Hippolyta, Emilia.

PIRITHOUS.
   No further.
HIPPOLYTA.   Sir, farewell. Repeat my wishes

---

   95. *what*] whatsoever, any.
   96. *Thirds*] reduces to a third of itself.
   97–98. *When . . . about*] "when his mind is clogged with a consciousness
that he fights in a bad cause" (Mason).
   103. *bounded*] ordained.
   106. *intelligence of state*] news concerning the state.
   106–107. *in . . . With*] at the same moment as.
   112. *Our . . . hearts*] if our hearts are not in the action we are engaged in.
   113. *event*] outcome.

To our great lord, of whose success I dare not
Make any timorous question; yet I wish him
Excess and overflow of power, and't might be,
To dure ill-dealing fortune. Speed to him;   5
Store never hurts good governors.
PIRITHOUS.   Though I know
His ocean needs not my poor drops, yet they
Must yield their tribute there. —My precious maid,
Those best affections that the heavens infuse
In their best-temper'd pieces keep enthron'd   10
In your dear heart.
EMILIA.   Thanks, sir. Remember me
To our all-royal brother, for whose speed
The great Bellona I'll solicit, and
Since in our terrene state petitions are not
Without gifts understood, I'll offer to her   15
What I shall be advised she likes. Our hearts
Are in his army, in his tent.
HIPPOLYTA.   In's bosom.
We have been soldiers and we cannot weep
When our friends don their helms, or put to sea,
Or tell of babes broach'd on the lance, or women   20
That have sod their infants in—and after ate them—
The brine they wept at killing 'em: then if
You stay to see of us such spinsters, we

---

5. *dure*] endure.

5. *Speed*] success.

6. *Store . . . governors*] Plenty does no harm to a good manager; Tilley, S 903.

10. *best-temper'd pieces*] most perfect works; alluding to the idea that character derived from the proportion in which the bodily humors were mixed.

14. *terrene*] earthly.

20. *broach'd*] spitted.

20–22. *or women . . . 'em*] The obscurity arises from the inversion of the parenthetical phrase *and after ate them*, which would more normally follow *killing 'em*.

21. *sod*] boiled.

23. *stay*] wait.

23. *spinsters*] spinners; women engaged in their usual peaceful occupations, by contrast with the Amazons, Hippolyta and Emilia; see l. 18.

       Should hold you here forever.
PIRITHOUS.   Peace be to you
       As I pursue this war, which shall be then   25
       Beyond further requiring.   *Exit* Pirithous.
EMILIA.   How his longing
       Follows his friend! Since his depart, his sports,
       Though craving seriousness and skill, pass'd slightly
       His careless execution, where nor gain
       Made him regard or loss consider, but   30
       Playing one business in his hand, another
       Directing in his head, his mind nurse equal
       To these so diff'ring twins. Have you observ'd him
       Since our great lord departed?
HIPPOLYTA.   With much labor;
       And I did love him for't. They two have cabin'd   35
       In many as dangerous as poor a corner,
       Peril and want contending; they have skiff'd
       Torrents, whose roaring tyranny and power
       I'th' least of these was dreadful; and they have
       Fought out together, where death's self was lodg'd;   40
       Yet fate hath brought them off. Their knot of love,
       Tied, weav'd, entangled, with so true, so long,
       And with a finger of so deep a cunning,
       May be outworn, never undone. I think
       Theseus cannot be umpire to himself,   45
       Cleaving his conscience into twain and doing
       Each side like justice, which he loves best.
EMILIA.   Doubtless
       There is a best, and reason has no manners

31. one] *Mason;* ore *Q.*

   24–26. *Peace . . . requiring*] "Peace be to you as long as I pursue this
war; when that is ended we shall not need to pray for it" (Mason).
   27. *his depart*] the departure of Theseus.
   35. *cabin'd*] taken shelter; *cabin*=a soldier's tent.
   37. *skiff'd*] crossed in a small boat.
   39. *I'th' . . . dreadful*] were dreadful at their mildest; referring to *tyranny
and power.*
   39–41. *and . . . off*] probably alluding to the most celebrated exploit of
Theseus and Pirithous, their descent to Hades to abduct Proserpina;
Ovid *Metamorphoses* xii. 210–244.
   43. *so . . . cunning*] such subtle art.
   47. *which*] Pirithous or Hippolyta.

To say it is not you. I was acquainted
Once with a time when I enjoy'd a playfellow;   50
You were at wars when she the grave enrich'd,
Who made too proud the bed; took leave o'th' moon—
Which then look'd pale at parting—when our count
Was each eleven.
HIPPOLYTA   'Twas Flavina.
EMILIA.   Yes.
You talk of Pirithous' and Theseus' love: 55
Theirs has more ground, is more maturely season'd,
More buckled with strong judgment, and their needs
The one of th'other may be said to water
Their intertangled roots of love; but I
And she I sigh and spoke of, were things innocent,   60
Lov'd for we did, and, like the elements,
That know not what, nor why, yet do effect
Rare issues by their operance, our souls
Did so to one another. What she lik'd
Was then of me approv'd, what not, condemn'd,   65
No more arraignment: the flower that I would pluck
And put between my breasts—O then but beginning
To swell about the blossom— she would long
Till she had such another, and commit it
To the like innocent cradle, where, phoenix-like,   70
They died in perfume; on my head no toy

---

54. eleven] *F;* a eleven *Q.*   Hearses ready with Palamon: and
54. Flavina] *1750; Flauia Q.*   Arcite: the 3. Queenes. Theseus:
58-64.] *Q prints marginal S.D.:* 2.   and his Lordes ready.

---

52. *moon*] emblem of chastity; cf. V.i.137-173.

53. *count*] age.

57. *buckled*] joined.

61. *for*] because.

61. *elements*] the four basic substances, earth, water, air, and fire.

63. *Rare issues*] wonderful results.

63. *operance*] operation.

66. *arraignment*] formal accusation.

70-71. *phoenix-like . . . perfume*] *phoenix:* "a mythical bird, of gorgeous plumage, fabled to be the only one of its kind, and to live five or six hundred years in the Arabian desert, after which it burnt itself to ashes on a funeral pile of aromatic twigs . . . only to emerge from its ashes with renewed youth" (*OED*).

71. *toy*] ornament.

But was her pattern; her affections—pretty,
Though happily her careless wear—I followed
For my most serious decking; had mine ear
Stol'n some new air or at adventure humm'd one   75
From musical coinage, why, it was a note
Whereon her spirits would sojourn—rather dwell on—
And sing it in her slumbers. This rehearsal—
Which ev'ry innocent wots well, comes in
Like old importment's bastard—has this end,   80
That the true love 'tween maid and maid may be
More than in sex dividual.

HIPPOLYTA.   Y'are out of breath,
And this high-speeded pace is but to say
That you shall never—like the maid Flavina—
Love any that's call'd man.   85

EMILIA.
I am sure I shall not.

HIPPOLYTA.   Now alack, weak sister,
I must no more believe thee in this point—
Though in't I know thou dost believe thyself—
Than I will trust a sickly appetite,
That loathes even as it longs. But sure, my sister,   90
If I were ripe for your persuasion, you
Have said enough to shake me from the arm
Of the all-noble Theseus, for whose fortunes
I will now in and kneel, with great assurance

73. happily . . . wear] *1750 conj.;*   79. ev'ry innocent] *Lamb;* fury-
happely, her careles, were *Q.*   innocent *Q;* surely innocence *1750*
75. one] *1750 conj.;* on *Q.*   *conj.*
76. musical] *F;* misicall *Q.*   82. dividual] *1750;* individuall *Q.*

---

72. *But was*] that was not.
72. *affections*] fancies.
73. *happily*] perhaps.
74. *decking*] adornment.
75. *air*] tune.
75–76. *at . . . coinage*] happened to compose one while humming.
78–80. *This . . . bastard*] "This description (of our love)—which any
innocent knows is but a feeble counterpart of the old passion (*emportement*)"
(Herford). As Herford noted, "significance" was a more usual meaning
of *importment*.
82. *in sex dividual*] between the sexes.
91. *ripe . . . persuasion*] ready to adopt your belief.

That we, more than his Pirithous, possess   95
The high throne in his heart.

EMILIA.   I am not
Against your faith, yet I continue mine.   *Exeunt.*

[I.iv]

Cornets. A battle struck within; then a retreat; flourish. [Palamon and Arcite brought in on two hearses.] Then enter Theseus, *victor [, with* Herald *and attendants]. The three* Queens *meet him and fall on their faces before him.*

FIRST QUEEN.
To thee no star be dark.

SECOND QUEEN.   Both heaven and earth
Friend thee forever.

THIRD QUEEN.   All the good that may
Be wish'd upon thy head, I cry amen to't.

THESEUS.
Th'impartial gods, who from the mounted heavens
View us their mortal herd, behold who err   5
And in their time chastise. Go and find out
The bones of your dead lords and honor them
With treble ceremony: rather than a gap
Should be in their dear rites, we would supply't.
But those we will depute which shall invest   10
You in your dignities and even each thing
Our haste does leave imperfect. So adieu,
And heaven's good eyes look on you.
                            Exeunt Queens [*with attendants*].

HERALD.   What are those?
Men of great quality, as may be judg'd

96–97.] *Q lines end:* heart/faith/   13.S.D.] *Q prints after* those.
mine.

0.1. *Cornets*] woodwind instruments, used particularly in the indoor private theaters.

1. *dark*] invisible; hence, ill-omened.

4. *mounted*] high.

4–6. *Th'impartial . . . chastise*] "God stays long but strikes at last," Tilley, G 224.

11. *even*] complete (verb).

12. *imperfect*] unfinished.

14. *quality*] rank.

By their appointment. Some of Thebes have told's   15
They are sisters' children, nephews to the king.

THESEUS.

By th' helm of Mars, I saw them in the war,
Like to a pair of lions smear'd with prey,
Make lanes in troops aghast. I fix'd my note
Constantly on them, for they were a mark   20
Worth a god's view. What prisoner was't that told me
When I enquired their names?

HERALD.   Wi' leave, they're called
Arcite and Palamon.

THESEUS.   'Tis right; those, those.
They are not dead?

HERALD.

Nor in a state of life. Had they been taken   25
When their last hurts were given, 'twas possible
They might have been recovered. Yet they breathe
And have the name of men.

THESEUS.   Then like men use 'em:
The very lees of such, millions of rates,
Exceed the wine of others. All our surgeons   30
Convent in their behoof; our richest balms,
Rather than niggard, waste; their lives concern us
Much more than Thebes is worth. Rather than have 'em
Freed of this plight and in their morning state,
Sound and at liberty, I would 'em dead;   35
But forty thousand fold we had rather have 'em

18. smear'd] *Q* (*corr.*); succard (*uncorr.*).
22. Wi' leave] *Dyce 1846;* We leave *Q;* We 'lieve *Littledale conj.*
26.] *Q prints marginal S.D.:* 3. Hearses ready.

---

15. *appointment*] arms and armor.
19. *note*] attention.
20. *mark*] sight.
24–25.] cf. *Knight's Tale,* l. 1015: "Nat fully quyke, ne fully dede they were."
29. *lees*] dregs.
29. *rates*] times.
31. *Convent*] summon.
31. *in their behoof*] for their benefit.
32. *niggard*] spend grudgingly.

Prisoners to us, than death. Bear 'em speedily
From our kind air, to them unkind, and minister
What man to man may do; for our sake, more,
Since I have known frights, fury, friends' behests,   40
Love's provocations, zeal, a mistress' task,
Desire of liberty, a fever, madness,
Hath set a mark which nature could not reach to
Without some imposition, sickness in will
O'er-wrestling strength in reason. For our love   45
And great Apollo's mercy, all our best
Their best skill tender. —Lead into the city,
Where having bound things scatter'd, we will post
To Athens 'fore our army.   *Flourish. Exeunt.*

[I.v]

Music. Enter the Queens *with the hearses of their knights, in a funeral solemnity, etc.*

> Urns and odors, bring away,
> Vapors, sighs, darken the day;
> Our dole more deadly looks than dying:

39. do;] *1750;* no punct. in *Q*.	45. O'er-wrestling] *Bertram;* Or
40. friends'] *Weber;* friends, *Q*.	wrastling *Q*.
41. Love's] *Weber;* Loves, *Q*.	49. 'fore] *1750;* for *Q*.

37–45. *Bear . . . reason*] The general sense of this difficult passage is that Theseus is the more disposed to treat the cousins kindly because his own experience suggests to him that they have fought for Creon only for emotional reasons, in spite of their better judgment; see I.ii.95–103.

38. *our kind air*] "Fresh air is ill for the wounded man," Tilley, A 93. Theseus' phrase suggests that the battle was fought near Athens, not at Thebes. In dramatic terms, this inconsistency prepares for the rapid return of Theseus to Athens.

41. *zeal*] religious enthusiasm.

43. *set a mark*] fixed a target.

43. *nature*] physical power.

44. *imposition*] (1) command, compulsion; (2) imposture, i.e., preference for false values before true.

45. *O'er-wrestling*] overcoming.

46. *And . . . mercy*] Apollo is invoked as god of healing.

[I.v]

3. *dole*] mourning.

Balms and gums and heavy cheers,
Sacred vials fill'd with tears,   5
And clamors through the wild air flying.

Come all sad and solemn shows,
That are quick-eyed pleasure's foes;
We convent nought else but woes.
We convent, etc.   10

THIRD QUEEN.

This funeral path brings to your household's grave:
Joy seize on you again! Peace sleep with him!

SECOND QUEEN.

And this to yours.

FIRST QUEEN.   Yours this way. Heavens lend
A thousand differing ways to one sure end.

THIRD QUEEN.

This world's a city full of straying streets,   15
And death's the marketplace, where each one meets.

Exeunt severally.

[II.i]   *Enter* Jailer *and* Wooer.

JAILER.

I may depart with little, while I live; something I may cast
to you, not much. Alas, the prison I keep, though it be for
great ones, yet they seldom come; before one salmon, you
shall take a number of minnows. I am given out to be better
lin'd than it can appear to me report is a true speaker. I   5

II.i] *Whole scene arranged as verse in Q.*

---

4. *cheers*] faces; appearance.
9. *convent*] (1) assemble, cf. I.iv.31; (2) suit.
13–16. *Heavens . . . meets.* Tilley, D 140, W 176; see also *Knight's Tale*,
ll. 2847–2849: "This world nys but a thurghfare ful of wo, And we been
pilgrymes, passynge to and fro. Deeth is an ende of every worldly soore."
15. *straying*] wandering.
16.1. *severally*] separately.
[II.i]
1. *depart*] part.
1. *cast*] give.
4–5. *better lin'd*] wealthier.

would I were really that I am deliver'd to be. Marry, what
I have—be it what it will—I will assure upon my daughter
at the day of my death.

WOOER.

Sir, I demand no more than your own offer, and I will
estate your daughter in what I have promised.   10

JAILER.

Well, we will talk more of this when the solemnity is past.
But have you a full promise of her? When that shall be seen,
I tender my consent.

    Enter [Jailer's] Daughter.

WOOER.

I have, sir. Here she comes.

JAILER.

Your friend and I have chanced to name you here, upon   15
the old business; but no more of that now. So soon as the
court hurry is over we will have an end of it. I'th' meantime
look tenderly to the two prisoners. I can tell you they are
princes.

DAUGHTER.

These strewings are for their chamber. 'Tis pity they are in   20
prison, and 'twere pity they should be out. I do think they
have patience to make any adversity asham'd; the prison
itself is proud of 'em, and they have all the world in their
chamber.

JAILER.

They are fam'd to be a pair of absolute men.   25

DAUGHTER.

By my troth, I think fame but stammers 'em; they stand a
grece above the reach of report.

JAILER.

I heard them reported in the battle to be the only doers.

DAUGHTER.

Nay most likely, for they are noble sufferers. I marvel how
they would have look'd had they been victors, that with   30

13.1.] *Q prints after* her?   16. that now.] *Colman;* that. Now,
                  Q.

20. *strewings*] rushes to strew on the floor.
26. *fame . . . 'em*] report does them less than justice.
27. *grece*] step.

such a constant nobility enforce a freedom out of bondage,
making misery their mirth and affliction a toy to jest at.

JAILER.

Do they so?

DAUGHTER.

It seems to me they have no more sense of their captivity
than I of ruling Athens. They eat well, look merrily, dis-   35
course of many things, but nothing of their own restraint
and disasters. Yet sometime a divided sigh, martyr'd as
'twere i'th' deliverance, will break from one of them; when
the other presently gives it so sweet a rebuke that I could
wish myself a sigh to be so chid, or at least a sigher to be   40
comforted.

WOOER.

I never saw 'em.

JAILER.

The duke himself came privately in the night, and so did
they. What the reason of it is, I know not.

                    Enter Palamon *and* Arcite *above.*

Look, yonder they are. That's Arcite looks out.   45

DAUGHTER.

No sir, no, that's Palamon. Arcite is the lower of the twain;
you may perceive a part of him.

JAILER.

Go to, leave your pointing. They would not make us their
object. Out of their sight!

DAUGHTER.

It is a holiday to look on them. Lord, the difference of men!   50

                                                    Exeunt.

[II.ii]   [Palamon *and* Arcite *remain.*]

PALAMON.

How do you, noble cousin?

ARCITE.   How do you, sir?

44.1.] *Q prints after* night.   0.1.] *Enter Palamon, and Arcite in
                                      prison. Q.*

---

36. *restraint*] imprisonment.
47. *perceive . . . him,*] see Introduction, p. xxvi, and textual note on
II.ii. 0.1.
48–49. *They . . . object*] They do not want to look at us.

−32−

PALAMON.

    Why, strong enough to laugh at misery
    And bear the chance of war; yet we are prisoners
    I fear forever, cousin.

ARCITE.   I believe it,
    And to that destiny have patiently   5
    Laid up my hour to come.

PALAMON.   O cousin Arcite,
    Where is Thebes now? Where is our noble country?
    Where are our friends and kindreds? Never more
    Must we behold those comforts, never see
    The hardy youths strive for the games of honor,   10
    Hung with the painted favors of their ladies,
    Like tall ships under sail; then start amongst 'em
    And, as an east wind, leave 'em all behind us,
    Like lazy clouds, whilst Palamon and Arcite,
    Even in the wagging of a wanton leg,   15
    Outstripp'd the people's praises, won the garlands
    Ere they have time to wish 'em ours. O never
    Shall we two exercise, like twins of honor,
    Our arms again and feel our fiery horses
    Like proud seas under us. Our good swords, now—   20
    Better the red-eyed god of war ne'er wore—
    Ravish'd our sides, like age must run to rust
    And deck the temples of those gods that hate us:
    These hands shall never draw 'em out like lightning
    To blast whole armies more.

ARCITE.   No, Palamon,   25
    Those hopes are prisoners with us. Here we are
    And here the graces of our youths must wither,
    Like a too-timely spring. Here age must find us
    And, which is heaviest, Palamon, unmarried:
    The sweet embraces of a loving wife,   30

21. wore] *1750;* were *Q.*   22. Ravish'd] *1750;* Bravishd *Q.*

5–6. *And . . . come*] and am reconciled to spending the remainder of
my life as a prisoner.
  10. *games*] victory in a contest.
  22. *Ravish'd*] snatched from.
  25. *blast*] ruin.

Loaden with kisses, arm'd with thousand cupids,
Shall never clasp our necks; no issue know us;
No figures of ourselves shall we e'er see
To glad our age, and, like young eagles, teach 'em
Boldly to gaze against bright arms, and say   35
"Remember what your fathers were, and conquer!"
The fair-eyed maids shall weep our banishments
And in their songs curse ever-blinded fortune,
Till she for shame see what a wrong she has done
To youth and nature. This is all our world: 40
We shall know nothing here but one another;
Hear nothing but the clock that tells our woes;
The vine shall grow, but we shall never see it;
Summer shall come and with her all delights,
But dead-cold winter must inhabit here still.   45

PALAMON.

'Tis too true, Arcite. To our Theban hounds
That shook the aged forest with their echoes,
No more now must we hallow; no more shake
Our pointed javelins, whilst the angry swine
Flies like a Parthian quiver from our rages,   50
Struck with our well-steel'd darts. All valiant uses—
The food and nourishment of noble minds—
In us two here shall perish; we shall die—
Which is the curse of honor—lastly,
Children of grief and ignorance.

ARCITE.   Yet cousin,   55
Even from the bottom of these miseries,
From all that fortune can inflict upon us,
I see two comforts rising, two mere blessings,
If the gods please; to hold here a brave patience,
And the enjoying of our griefs together.   60

---

33. *figures*] images.
34–35. *like . . . arms*] "Only the eagle can gaze at the sun," Tilley, E 3.
42. *tells*] counts.
48. *hallow*] shout.
50. *Parthian quiver*] *Parthian*, because in flight; Tilley, P 80: "The Parthians fight flying away"; *quiver*, because full of javelins.
51. *uses*] pursuits.
58. *mere*] unmixed.

Whilst Palamon is with me, let me perish
If I think this our prison.
PALAMON.   Certainly
'Tis a main goodness, cousin, that our fortunes
Were twin'd together. 'Tis most true, two souls
Put in two noble bodies, let 'em suffer   65
The gall of hazard, so they grow together,
Will never sink; they must not, say they could.
A willing man dies sleeping and all's done.
ARCITE.
Shall we make worthy uses of this place
That all men hate so much?
PALAMON.   How, gentle cousin?   70
ARCITE.
Let's think this prison holy sanctuary,
To keep us from corruption of worse men:
We are young and yet desire the ways of honor,
That liberty and common conversation,
The poison of pure spirits, might, like women,   75
Woo us to wander from. What worthy blessing
Can be, but our imaginations
May make it ours? And here being thus together,
We are an endless mine to one another;
We are one another's wife, ever begetting   80
New births of love; we are father, friends, acquaintance;
We are in one another, families;
I am your heir and you are mine; this place
Is our inheritance: no hard oppressor
Dare take this from us; here, with a little patience,   85
We shall live long and loving. No surfeits seek us:
The hand of war hurts none here, nor the seas
Swallow their youth. Were we at liberty,
A wife might part us lawfully, or business;
Quarrels consume us; envy of ill men   90

---

66. *The . . . hazard*] the effects of misfortune.
66. *so*] provided that.
74. *common conversation*] indiscriminate social contact.
75. *like women*] as if we were women.
90–91. *envy . . . acquaintance*] we might come to feel envy towards bad men.

     Crave our acquaintance; I might sicken, cousin,
     Where you should never know it and so perish
     Without your noble hand to close mine eyes
     Or prayers to the gods. A thousand chances,
     Were we from hence, would sever us.

PALAMON.   You have made me—   95
     I thank you, cousin Arcite—almost wanton
     With my captivity. What a misery
     It is to live abroad and everywhere!
     'Tis like a beast, methinks. I find the court here—
     I am sure, a more content; and all those pleasures   100
     That woo the wills of men to vanity
     I see through now, and am sufficient
     To tell the world 'tis but a gaudy shadow,
     That old Time, as he passes by, takes with him.
     What had we been, old in the court of Creon,   105
     Where sin is justice, lust and ignorance
     The virtues of the great ones? Cousin Arcite,
     Had not the loving gods found this place for us,
     We had died as they do, ill old men, unwept,
     And had their epitaphs, the people's curses.   110
     Shall I say more?

ARCITE.   I would hear you still.

PALAMON.   Ye shall.
     Is there record of any two that lov'd
     Better than we do, Arcite?

ARCITE.   Sure there cannot.

PALAMON.
     I do not think it possible our friendship
     Should ever leave us.

ARCITE.   Till our deaths it cannot,   115

        Enter Emilia *and her* Woman.

     And after death our spirits shall be led
     To those that love eternally.   [Palamon *sees* Emilia *and is silent.*]
                   Speak on, sir.

96–97. *wanton With*] free from care about.
98. *abroad*] at large.
100. *more*] greater.

EMILIA.
This garden has a world of pleasures in't.
What flower is this?
WOMAN.   'Tis call'd Narcissus, madam.
EMILIA.
That was a fair boy, certain, but a fool   120
To love himself. Were there not maids enough?
ARCITE.
Pray forward.
PALAMON.   Yes.
EMILIA.   Or were they all hard-hearted?
WOMAN.
They could not be to one so fair.
EMILIA.   Thou wouldst not.
WOMAN.
I think I should not, madam.
EMILIA.   That's a good wench:
But take heed to your kindness, though.
WOMAN.   Why, madam?   125
EMILIA.
Men are mad things.
ARCITE.   Will ye go forward, cousin?
EMILIA.
Canst not thou work such flowers in silk, wench?
WOMAN.   Yes.
EMILIA.
I'll have a gown full of 'em, and of these.
This is a pretty color, will't not do
Rarely upon a skirt, wench?
WOMAN.   Dainty, madam.   130
ARCITE.
Cousin, cousin, how do you, sir? Why, Palamon!
PALAMON.
Never till now I was in prison, Arcite.
ARCITE.
Why what's the matter, man?
PALAMON.   Behold and wonder!

118.S.P.] *1750; Q prints before l.*
119.

___

119. *Narcissus*] see IV.ii.32; Ovid *Metamorphoses* iii. 339–510.

By heaven, she is a goddess!

ARCITE.   Ha!

PALAMON.   Do reverence;
She is a goddess, Arcite.

EMILIA.   Of all flowers,   135
Methinks a rose is best.

WOMAN.   Why, gentle madam?

EMILIA.
It is the very emblem of a maid:
For when the west wind courts her gently
How modestly she blows and paints the sun
With her chaste blushes! When the north comes near her, 140
Rude and impatient, then, like chastity,
She locks her beauties in her bud again
And leaves him to base briers.

WOMAN.   Yet, good madam,
Sometimes her modesty will blow so far
She falls for't: a maid,   145
If she have any honor, would be loth
To take example by her.

EMILIA.   Thou art wanton.

ARCITE.
She is wondrous fair.

PALAMON.   She is all the beauty extant.

EMILIA.
The sun grows high, let's walk in. Keep these flowers:
We'll see how near art can come near their colors.   150
I am wondrous merry-hearted, I could laugh now.

WOMAN.
I could lie down, I am sure.

EMILIA.   And take one with you?

WOMAN.
That's as we bargain, madam.

EMILIA.   Well, agree then.

                                Exeunt Emilia *and* Woman.

135–147.] cf. V.i.163–170.
139. *blows*] blooms.
151–152. *I could laugh . . . down*] Tilley, L 92: "Laugh and lie down";
originally the name of a card game, "Laugh and lay down." Frequently,
as here, with sexual innuendo.

PALAMON.

    What think you of this beauty?

ARCITE.   'Tis a rare one.

PALAMON.

    Is't but a rare one?

ARCITE.   Yes, a matchless beauty.   155

PALAMON.

    Might not a man well lose himself and love her?

ARCITE.

    I cannot tell what you have done: I have,

    Beshrew mine eyes for't. Now I feel my shackles.

PALAMON.

    You love her, then?

ARCITE.   Who would not?

PALAMON.   And desire her?

ARCITE.

    Before my liberty.   160

PALAMON.

    I saw her first.

ARCITE.   That's nothing.

PALAMON.   But it shall be.

ARCITE.

    I saw her too.

PALAMON.   Yes, but you must not love her.

ARCITE.

    I will not, as you do; to worship her,

    As she is heavenly and a blessed goddess.

    I love her as a woman, to enjoy her: 165

    So both may love.

PALAMON.

    You shall not love at all.

ARCITE.   Not love at all?

    Who shall deny me?

PALAMON.

    I, that first saw her; I, that took possession

    First with mine eye of all those beauties   170

    In her reveal'd to mankind. If thou lov'st her

---

171. *thou*] From this point Palamon's anger is reflected in his use of *thou* in place of the more polite and formal *you*.

Or entertain'st a hope to blast my wishes,
Thou art a traitor, Arcite, and a fellow
False as thy title to her: friendship, blood
And all the ties between us I disclaim,   175
If thou once think upon her.

ARCITE.   Yes, I love her,
And if the lives of all my name lay on it,
I must do so. I love her with my soul!
If that will lose ye, farewell Palamon.
I say again,   180
I love her, and in loving her maintain
I am as worthy and as free a lover,
And have as just a title to her beauty
As any Palamon, or any living
That is a man's son.

PALAMON.   Have I call'd thee friend?   185

ARCITE.
Yes, and have found me so. Why are you mov'd thus?
Let me deal coldly with you: am not I
Part of your blood, part of your soul? You have told me
That I was Palamon, and you were Arcite.

PALAMON.   Yes.

ARCITE.
Am not I liable to those affections,   190
Those joys, griefs, angers, fears, my friend shall suffer?

PALAMON.
Ye may be.

ARCITE.   Why then would you deal so cunningly,
So strangely, so unlike a noble kinsman,
To love alone? Speak truly, do you think me
Unworthy of her sight?

PALAMON.   No; but unjust   195
If thou pursue that sight.

ARCITE.   Because another
First sees the enemy, shall I stand still

180–181.] *one line in Q.*   188. your blood] *F;* you blood *Q.*
181. love her] *Walker;* love *Q.*

182. *free*] noble.
186. *mov'd thus*] so angry.
187. *coldly*] calmly.

And let mine honor down and never charge?
PALAMON.
    Yes, if he be but one.
ARCITE.   But say that one
    Had rather combat me?
PALAMON.   Let that one say so,   200
    And use thy freedom; else if thou pursuest her,
    Be as that cursed man that hates his country,
    A branded villain.
ARCITE.   You are mad.
PALAMON.   I must be:
    Till thou art worthy, Arcite, it concerns me;
    And in this madness if I hazard thee   205
    And take thy life, I deal but truly.
ARCITE.   Fie, sir,
    You play the child extremely. I will love her,
    I must, I ought to do so and I dare,
    And all this justly.
PALAMON.   O that now, that now
    Thy false self and thy friend had but this fortune,   210
    To be one hour at liberty and grasp
    Our good swords in our hands! I would quickly teach thee
    What 'twere to filch affection from another:
    Thou art baser in it than a cutpurse!
    Put but thy head out of this window more   215
    And, as I have a soul, I'll nail thy life to't.
ARCITE.
    Thou dar'st not, fool; thou canst not; thou art feeble.
    Put my head out? I'll throw my body out
    And leap the garden, when I see her next,
    And pitch between her arms to anger thee.   220

Enter Jailer.

PALAMON.
    No more, the keeper's coming. I shall live

220.1.] *Q prints after l. 219 and reads*
"Keeper" for "Jailer" in this scene.

---

  216. *to't*] i.e., to the window frame; cf. Introduction, p. xxvi.
  219. *leap*] jump into.
  220. *pitch*] (1) thrust in; (2) place myself.

−41−

To knock thy brains out with my shackles.
ARCITE.   Do.
JAILER.
    By your leave, gentlemen.
PALAMON.   Now, honest keeper?
JAILER.
    Lord Arcite, you must presently to th' duke:
    The cause I know not yet.
ARCITE.   I am ready, keeper.   225
JAILER.
    Prince Palamon, I must awhile bereave you
    Of your fair cousin's company.

                                    Exeunt Arcite *and* Jailer.
PALAMON.   And me too,
    Even when you please, of life. Why is he sent for?
    It may be he shall marry her; he's goodly,
    And like enough the duke hath taken notice   230
    Both of his blood and body. But his falsehood!
    Why should a friend be treacherous? If that
    Get him a wife so noble and so fair,
    Let honest men ne'er love again. Once more
    I would but see this fair one. Blessed garden,   235
    And fruit and flowers more blessed, that still blossom
    As her bright eyes shine on ye! Would I were,
    For all the fortune of my life hereafter,
    Yon little tree, yon blooming apricock;
    How I would spread and fling my wanton arms   240
    In at her window! I would bring her fruit
    Fit for the gods to feed on; youth and pleasure
    Still as she tasted should be doubled on her;
    And, if she be not heavenly, I would make her
    So near the gods in nature they should fear her: 245
    And then I am sure she would love me.

                            Enter Jailer.

                                    How now, keeper,
    Where's Arcite?
JAILER.   Banish'd. Prince Pirithous
246.S.D.] Q *prints after l. 245.*
_____
    243. *Still as*] whenever.

                            —42—

Obtained his liberty; but never more,
Upon his oath and life, must he set foot
Upon this kingdom.

PALAMON.   He's a blessed man!   250
He shall see Thebes again and call to arms
The bold young men that, when he bids 'em charge,
Fall on like fire. Arcite shall have a fortune,
If he dare make himself a worthy lover,
Yet in the field to strike a battle for her;   255
And if he lose her then, he's a cold coward!
How bravely may he bear himself to win her
If he be noble Arcite; thousand ways!
Were I at liberty, I would do things
Of such a virtuous greatness that this lady,   260
This blushing virgin, should take manhood to her
And seek to ravish me.

JAILER.   My lord, for you
I have this charge too.

PALAMON.   To discharge my life.

JAILER.
No, but from this place to remove your lordship;
The windows are too open.

PALAMON.   Devils take 'em   265
That are so envious to me! Prithee kill me.

JAILER.
And hang for't afterward.

PALAMON.   By this good light,
Had I a sword I would kill thee.

JAILER.   Why, my lord?

PALAMON.
Thou bring'st such pelting scurvy news continually,
Thou art not worthy life. I will not go.   270

JAILER.
Indeed you must, my lord.

PALAMON.   May I see the garden?

---

263. *charge*] order.
263. *discharge*] Palamon's punning reply depends on the second meaning
for *charge*, to "load a gun."
269. *pelting*] worthless.

JAILER.
   No.
PALAMON. Then I am resolv'd: I will not go.
JAILER.
   I must constrain you, then; and for you are dangerous,
   I'll clap more irons on you.
PALAMON.   Do, good keeper.
   I'll shake 'em so, ye shall not sleep;   275
   I'll make ye a new morris. Must I go?
JAILER.
   There is no remedy.
PALAMON.   Farewell, kind window,
   May rude wind never hurt thee. O my lady,
   If ever thou hast felt what sorrow was,
   Dream how I suffer. —Come, now bury me.   280
                          Exeunt Palamon *and* Jailer.

[II.iii]   *Enter* Arcite.

ARCITE.
   Banish'd the kingdom? 'Tis a benefit,
   A mercy I must thank 'em for; but banish'd
   The free enjoying of that face I die for,
   O 'twas a studied punishment, a death
   Beyond imagination; such a vengeance   5
   That, were I old and wicked, all my sins
   Could never pluck upon me. Palamon,
   Thou hast the start now; thou shalt stay and see
   Her bright eyes break each morning 'gainst thy window
   And let in life into thee; thou shalt feed   10
   Upon the sweetness of a noble beauty,
   That nature ne'er exceeded, nor ne'er shall.
   Good gods, what happiness has Palamon!

---

6. sins] Q (*corr.*); fins (*uncorr.*).

---

  273. *for*] because.
  276. *morris*] morris dance; see III.v.104.
  277. *There . . . remedy*] Tilley, R 71: "There is no remedy but patience."
[II.iii]
  4. *studied*] carefully contrived.
  4–5. *a death . . . imagination*] a worse death than could be imagined.

Twenty to one, he'll come to speak to her,
And if she be as gentle as she's fair,   15
I know she's his; he has a tongue will tame tempests
And make the wild rocks wanton. Come what can come,
The worst is death. I will not leave the kingdom;
I know mine own is but a heap of ruins,
And no redress there. If I go, he has her.   20
I am resolv'd another shape shall make me
Or end my fortunes. Either way I am happy:
I'll see her, and be near her or no more.

Enter four Country-people *and one with a garland before them.*

FIRST COUNTRYMAN.
    My masters, I'll be there, that's certain.
SECOND COUNTRYMAN.   And I'll be there.
THIRD COUNTRYMAN.   And I.
FOURTH COUNTRYMAN.
    Why then, have with ye, boys! 'Tis but a chiding: 25
    Let the plough play today, I'll tickle't out
    Of the jades' tails tomorrow.
FIRST COUNTRYMAN.   I am sure
    To have my wife as jealous as a turkey:
    But that's all one, I'll go through, let her mumble.
SECOND COUNTRYMAN.
    Clap her aboard tomorrow night and stow her,   30
    And all's made up again.
THIRD COUNTRYMAN.   Ay, do but put
    A fescue in her fist and you shall see her
    Take a new lesson out and be a good wench.

16.] *Q line ends:* tame.	(*uncorr.*).
23.1. *garland*] *Q* (*corr.*); *Garlon*	31–32. Ay . . . see her] *one line in Q.*

---

17. *Come . . . come*] Tilley, C 529.
21. *another shape*] disguise.
23. *no more*] i.c., be no more; die.
23.1 *garland*] for use in the May games; either as a prize or to be worn by the May queen.
25. *'Tis . . . chiding*] it will only mean a scolding.
30. *Clap her aboard*] board her.
32. *fescue*] pointer.
33. *Take . . . out*] learn a new lesson.

Do we all hold against the maying?

FOURTH COUNTRYMAN.   Hold?

What should ail us?

THIRD COUNTRYMAN.   Arcas will be there.

SECOND COUNTRYMAN.   And Sennois   35

And Rycas, and three better lads ne'er danc'd

Under green tree; and ye know what wenches, ha!

But will the dainty domine, the schoolmaster,

Keep touch, do you think? For he does all, ye know.

THIRD COUNTRYMAN.

He'll eat a horn-book ere he fail!   40

Go to, the matter's too far driven between

Him and the tanner's daughter to let slip now;

And she must see the duke, and she must dance too.

FOURTH COUNTRYMAN.

Shall we be lusty?

SECOND COUNTRYMAN.   All the boys in Athens

Blow wind i'th' breech on's! And here I'll be   45

And there I'll be, for our town, and here again,

And there again. Ha, boys, hey for the weavers!

FIRST COUNTRYMAN.

This must be done i'th' woods.

FOURTH COUNTRYMAN.   O, pardon me—

SECOND COUNTRYMAN.

By any means, our thing of learning says so;

36–60.] *mainly arranged as prose in Q.*   49. says] *1750;* sees *Q.*
37. ye] *1750;* yet *Q.*

---

34. *Do . . . maying*] Do we all still mean to take part in the maying?

35. *Arcas*] in classical mythology, the name of the legendary founder of Arcadia; also a name of the god Mercury.

38. *domine*] schoolmaster.

39. *Keep touch*] keep his promise.

40. *horn-book*] the first schoolbook, a single leaf containing the alphabet, the digits, and the Lord's Prayer and covered with a sheet of transparent horn.

44. *lusty*] merry.

45. *Blow . . . on's*] i.e., cannot compete with us; cf. Beaumont, *Knight of the Burning Pestle*, I.62: "If any of them all blow winde in the taile on him, Il'e be hang'd."

45. *on's*] of us.

49. *thing of learning*] man of learning, probably contemptuous.

Where he himself will edify the duke most parlously   50
In our behalfs: he's excellent i'th' woods,
Bring him to th' plains, his learning makes no cry.

THIRD COUNTRYMAN.

We'll see the sports, then every man to's tackle!
And, sweet companions, let's rehearse, by any means,
Before the ladies see us, and do sweetly,   55
And god knows what may come on't!

FOURTH COUNTRYMAN.   Content: the sports
Once ended, we'll perform. Away boys, and hold!

ARCITE.

By your leaves, honest friends; pray you, whither go you?

FOURTH COUNTRYMAN.   Whither?
Why what a question's that?

ARCITE.   Yes, 'tis a question
To me, that know not.

THIRD COUNTRYMAN.   To the games, my friend.   60

SECOND COUNTRYMAN.

Where were you bred, you know it not?

ARCITE.   Not far, sir.
Are there such games today?

FIRST COUNTRYMAN.   Yes marry, are there,
And such as you never saw. The duke himself
Will be in person there.

ARCITE.   What pastimes are they?

SECOND COUNTRYMAN.

Wrestling and running. —'Tis a pretty fellow.   65

THIRD COUNTRYMAN.

Thou wilt not go along?

ARCITE.   Not yet, sir.

FOURTH COUNTRYMAN.   Well, sir,
Take your own time. —Come, boys.

FIRST COUNTRYMAN.   My mind misgives me:
This fellow has a vengeance trick o'th' hip;
Mark how his body's made for't.

SECOND COUNTRYMAN.   I'll be hang'd though

---

50. *edify*] instruct.
52. *makes no cry*] is silent; has no effect.
53. *tackle*] equipment for the morris dance; Tilley, T 7, "To stand to
one's tackling," to be ready for action.

If he dare venture; hang him plum porridge!   70
He wrestle? He roast eggs! Come, let's be gone, lads.
                              Exeunt four [Countrymen].

ARCITE.

This is an offer'd opportunity
I durst not wish for. Well I could have wrestled,
The best men call'd it excellent; and run
Swifter than wind upon a field of corn,   75
Curling the wealthy ears, never flew. I'll venture,
And in some poor disguise be there. Who knows
Whether my brows may not be girt with garlands,
And happiness prefer me to a place
Where I may ever dwell in sight of her?   *Exit* Arcite.   80

[II.iv]   *Enter* Jailer's Daughter *alone*.

DAUGHTER.

Why should I love this gentleman? 'Tis odds
He never will affect me: I am base,
My father the mean keeper of his prison,
And he a prince. To marry him is hopeless,
To be his whore is witless. Out upon't,   5
What pushes are we wenches driven to
When fifteen once has found us! First I saw him;
I, seeing, thought he was a goodly man;
He has as much to please a woman in him—
If he please to bestow it so—as ever   10
These eyes yet look'd on; next, I pitied him,

73. Well] *1750;* Well, *Q.*

---

70. *plum porridge*] thick broth made of beef, dried fruits, white bread, spices, wine, and sugar; eaten at Christmas.

71. *He wrestle . . . eggs*] Herford cites "Set a fool to roast eggs, and a wise man to eat them" as proverbial.

73. *I could have*] cf. II.v.11 and note.

76. *never*] intensifies the negative already implied in *Swifter*; E. A. Abbott, *A Shakespearian Grammar* (London, 1872), §406.

79. *happiness*] success.

[II.iv]

2. *affect*] love.

2. *base*] of humble birth.

6. *pushes*] efforts.

7. *fifteen*] cf. V.i.130, V.ii.30.

And so would any young wench, o'my conscience,
That ever dream'd, or vow'd her maidenhead
To a young handsome man; then I lov'd him,
Extremely lov'd him, infinitely lov'd him;   15
And yet he had a cousin, fair as he too;
But in my heart was Palamon and there,
Lord, what a coil he keeps! To hear him
Sing in an evening, what a heaven it is!
And yet his songs are sad ones. Fairer spoken   20
Was never gentleman: when I come in
To bring him water in a morning, first
He bows his noble body, then salutes me, thus:
"Fair, gentle maid, good morrow; may thy goodness
Get thee a happy husband." Once he kiss'd me: 25
I lov'd my lips the better ten days after;
Would he would do so ev'ry day! He grieves much,
And me as much to see his misery.
What should I do to make him know I love him?
For I would fain enjoy him. Say I ventur'd   30
To set him free? What says the law then? Thus much
For law or kindred! I will do it,
And this night or tomorrow he shall love me.   *Exit.*

[II.v]

This short flourish of cornets and shouts within. Enter Theseus, Hippolyta,
Pirithous, Emilia, Arcite [*disguised as a countryman*] *with a garland*
[*and attendants*].

THESEUS.
    You have done worthily; I have not seen,
    Since Hercules, a man of tougher sinews.
    Whate'er you are, you run the best and wrestle
    That these times can allow.
ARCITE.   I am proud to please you.

II.v.] Scaena 4. *Q.*   0.1. *This . . . within*] *Q* *prints in*
                                          margin.

_____

  18. *coil he keeps*] turmoil he makes; Tilley, C 505.
  30. *fain*] gladly.
[II.v]
  4. *That . . . allow*] that can exist in the present age.

THESEUS.
   What country bred you?
ARCITE.   This; but far off, prince.   5
THESEUS.
   Are you a gentleman?
ARCITE.   My father said so,
   And to those gentle uses gave me life.
THESEUS.
   Are you his heir?
ARCITE.   His youngest, sir.
THESEUS.   Your father
   Sure is a happy sire, then. What proves you?
ARCITE.
   A little of all noble qualities.   10
   I could have kept a hawk and well have hallow'd
   To a deep cry of dogs; I dare not praise
   My feat in horsemanship, yet they that knew me
   Would say it was my best piece; last, and greatest,
   I would be thought a soldier.
THESEUS.   You are perfect.   15
PIRITHOUS.
   Upon my soul, a proper man.
EMILIA.   He is so.
PIRITHOUS.
   How do you like him, lady?
HIPPOLYTA.   I admire him:
   I have not seen so young a man so noble—
   If he say true—of his sort.
EMILIA.   Believe,
   His mother was a wondrous handsome woman;   20

---

   7. *gentle uses*] honorable employments.
   9. *sire*] dissyllabic.
   9. *proves you*] shows that you are what you claim to be.
   10. *qualities*] skills.
   11. *I could have*] I knew how to; a common locution in Fletcher, cf.
II.iii.73.
   13. *feat*] skill.
   14. *piece*] part, ability.
   16. *proper*] handsome.
   19. *sort*] rank.
   19. *Believe*] i.e., believe me; cf. IV.i.47.

His face, methinks, goes that way.

HIPPOLYTA.   But his body
And fiery mind illustrate a brave father.

PIRITHOUS.
Mark how his virtue, like a hidden sun,
Breaks through his baser garments.

HIPPOLYTA.   He's well got, sure.

THESEUS.
What made you seek this place, sir?

ARCITE.   Noble Theseus,   25
To purchase name and do my ablest service
To such a well-found wonder as thy worth;
For only in thy court, of all the world,
Dwells fair-eyed honor.

PIRITHOUS.   All his words are worthy.

THESEUS.
Sir, we are much indebted to your travel,   30
Nor shall you lose your wish. —Pirithous,
Dispose of this fair gentleman.

PIRITHOUS   Thanks, Theseus.—
What'er you are, y'are mine and I shall give you
To a most noble service, to this lady,
This bright young virgin; pray observe her goodness.   35
You have honor'd her fair birthday with your virtues
And, as your due, y'are hers. Kiss her fair hand, sir.

ARCITE.
Sir, y'are a noble giver. —Dearest beauty,
Thus let me seal my vow'd faith. When your servant,
Your most unworthy creature, but offends you,   40
Command him die, he shall.

EMILIA.   That were too cruel.
If you deserve well, sir, I shall soon see't.
Y'are mine, and somewhat better than your rank I'll use you.

---

22. *illustrate . . . father*] give clear evidence that he had a brave father.
27. *well-found*] well furnished.
30. *travel*] effort, both in coming to the court of Theseus and in winning the games.
32. *Dispose of*] take charge of.

PIRITHOUS.

    I'll see you furnish'd, and because you say

    You are a horseman, I must needs entreat you   45

    This afternoon to ride, but 'tis a rough one.

ARCITE.

    I like him better, prince; I shall not then

    Freeze in my saddle.

THESEUS.   Sweet, you must be ready,—

    And you, Emilia—and you, friend—and all,

    Tomorrow by the sun, to do observance   50

    To flow'ry May in Dian's wood. —Wait well, sir,

    Upon your mistress. —Emily, I hope

    He shall not go afoot.

EMILIA.   That were a shame, sir,

    While I have horses. —Take your choice; and what

    You want at any time, let me but know it.   55

    If you serve faithfully, I dare assure you

    You'll find a loving mistress.

ARCITE.   If I do not,

    Let me find that my father ever hated,

    Disgrace and blows.

THESEUS.   Go lead the way; you have won it.

    It shall be so: you shall receive all dues   60

    Fit for the honor you have won, 'twere wrong else.—

    Sister, beshrew my heart, you have a servant,

    That, if I were a woman, would be master:

    But you are wise.

EMILIA.   I hope, too wise for that, sir.

                           Flourish. Exeunt omnes.

[II.vi]   *Enter* Jailer's Daughter *alone.*

DAUGHTER.

    Let all the dukes and all the devils roar,

    He is at liberty. I have ventur'd for him,

    And out I have brought him. To a little wood

---

44. *furnish'd*] provided.

53–54. *That . . . horses*] cf. V.iv.49–50.

55. *want*] lack.

A mile hence I have sent him, where a cedar,
Higher than all the rest, spreads like a plane,   5
Fast by a brook; and there he shall keep close
Till I provide him files and food, for yet
His iron bracelets are not off. O love,
What a stout-hearted child thou art! My father
Durst better have endur'd cold iron than done it.   10
I love him beyond love and beyond reason,
Or wit, or safety. I have made him know it:
I care not, I am desperate; if the law
Find me and then condemn me for't, some wenches,
Some honest-hearted maids, will sing my dirge   15
And tell to memory my death was noble,
Dying almost a martyr. That way he takes,
I purpose is my way too. Sure, he cannot
Be so unmanly as to leave me here?
If he do, maids will not so easily   20
Trust men again. And yet he has not thank'd me
For what I have done; no, not so much as kiss'd me;
And that, methinks, is not so well: nor scarcely
Could I persuade him to become a freeman,
He made such scruples of the wrong he did   25
To me and to my father. Yet I hope,
When he considers more, this love of mine
Will take more root within him. Let him do
What he will with me, so he use me kindly,
For use me so he shall or I'll proclaim him,   30
And to his face, no man. I'll presently
Provide him necessaries and pack my clothes up,
And where there is a path of ground I'll venture,
So he be with me; by him, like a shadow,
I'll ever dwell. Within this hour the hubbub   35
Will be all o'er the prison: I am then
Kissing the man they look for! Farewell, father;

12. it:] *Colman; no punct. in Q.*   15. dirge] *1711;* Dirge. *Q.*

10. *cold iron*] manacles.
12. *wit*] sense.
29. *kindly*] (1) benevolently; (2) sexually, according to nature.
33. *of*] on.

Get many more such prisoners, and such daughters,
And shortly you may keep yourself. Now to him!　　　　*[Exit.]*

[III.i]
Cornets in sundry places. Noise and hallowing as people a-Maying. Enter
Arcite *alone.*

ARCITE.

The duke has lost Hippolyta; each took
A several land. This is a solemn rite
They owe bloom'd May, and the Athenians pay it
To th' heart of ceremony. O Queen Emilia,
Fresher than May, sweeter　　　　　　　　　　　　　　　5
Than her gold buttons on the boughs, or all
Th'enamell'd knacks o'th' mead or garden, yea
We challenge too the bank of any nymph
That makes the stream seem flowers; thou, O jewel
O'th' wood, o'th' world, hast likewise blest a pace　　10
With thy sole presence. In thy rumination
That I, poor man, might eftsoons come between
And chop on some cold thought! Thrice blessed chance
To drop on such a mistress, expectation
Most guiltless on't. Tell me, O Lady Fortune,　　　　15
Next after Emily my sovereign, how far
I may be proud. She takes strong note of me,

0.1. *Cornets . . . a-Maying*] Q　　　11. presence.] *Colman;* presence, Q.
prints in margin between II.vi and　　13. thought!] *Colman;* thought, Q.
III.i.

---

　38. *Get*] (1) obtain; (2) beget.
　39. *keep yourself*] (1) be a prisoner in your own jail; (2) live alone.
[III.i]
　2. *several*] different.
　2. *land*] glade, clearing.
　6. *buttons*] buds.
　7. *enamell'd*] variously colored.
　7. *knacks*] ornaments; i.e., flowers.
　8. *nymph*] water spirit, here "river."
　10. *pace*] passage through woods.
　12. *eftsoons*] immediately.
　13. *chop on*] interrupt.
　13. *cold*] chaste.
　14–15. *expectation . . . on't*] without premeditation.
　15. *on't*] of it.

Hath made me near her, and this beauteous morn,
The prim'st of all the year, presents me with
A brace of horses: two such steeds might well   20
Be by a pair of kings back'd, in a field
That their crowns' titles tried. Alas, alas,
Poor cousin Palamon, poor prisoner, thou
So little dream'st upon my fortune that
Thou think'st thyself the happier thing, to be   25
So near Emilia: me thou deem'st at Thebes,
And therein wretched, although free; but if
Thou knew'st my mistress breath'd on me, and that
I ear'd her language, liv'd in her eye, O coz,
What passion would enclose thee.

Enter Palamon, *as out of a bush, with his shackles:* [*he*] *bends his fist at* Arcite.

PALAMON.   Traitor kinsman,   30
Thou shouldst perceive my passion, if these signs
Of prisonment were off me and this hand
But owner of a sword: by all oaths in one,
I and the justice of my love would make thee
A confess'd traitor. O thou most perfidious   35
That ever gently look'd, the void'st of honor
That e'er bore gentle token, falsest cousin
That ever blood made kin, call'st thou her thine?
I'll prove it in my shackles, with these hands,
Void of appointment, that thou liest and art   40
A very thief in love, a chaffy lord
Nor worth the name of villain. Had I a sword

20. horses:] *Colman;* horses, *Q.*   36. void'st] *1750;* voydes *Q.*
26. Emilia:] *1711; Emilia, Q.*   36. honor] *1711;* honour. *Q.*

19. *prim'st*] best.
21. *field*] battlefield.
29. *ear'd*] heard.
30. *passion*] anger.
36. *gently look'd*] looked like a gentleman.
37. *bore gentle token*] showed signs of gentility.
40. *Void of appointment*] without weapons.
41. *chaffy*] worthless.

    And these house clogs away—

ARCITE.   Dear cousin Palamon—

PALAMON.

    Cozener Arcite, give me language such

    As thou hast show'd me feat.

ARCITE.   Not finding in   45

    The circuit of my breast any gross stuff

    To form me like your blazon, holds me to

    This gentleness of answer: 'tis your passion

    That thus mistakes, the which, to you being enemy,

    Cannot to me be kind. Honor and honesty   50

    I cherish and depend on, howsoe'er

    You skip them in me, and with them, fair coz,

    I'll maintain my proceedings. Pray be pleas'd

    To show in generous terms your griefs, since that

    Your question's with your equal, who professes   55

    To clear his own way with the mind and sword

    Of a true gentleman.

PALAMON.   That thou durst, Arcite!

ARCITE.

    My coz, my coz, you have been well advertis'd

    How much I dare; y'have seen me use my sword

    Against th'advice of fear. Sure, of another   60

    You would not hear me doubted, but your silence

    Should break out, though i'th' sanctuary.

PALAMON.   Sir,

    I have seen you move in such a place which well

    Might justify your manhood; you were call'd

---

   43. *house clogs*] leg irons.

   44. *Cozener*] deceiver; the punning association with *cousin* is very common.

   44–45. *give . . . feat*] suit your words to your actions.

   45–47. *Not . . . blazon*] finding in my thoughts no baseness to make me fit your description.

   51. *depend on*] rely on.

   52. *skip*] pass over.

   55. *question*] dispute.

   57. *That thou durst*] if only you dared.

   58. *advertis'd*] warned.

   60. *of another*] by anyone else.

   62. *sanctuary*] a church or sacred place in which a fugitive from law was safe from arrest.

   64. *manhood*] courage.

A good knight and a bold. But the whole week's not fair 65
If any day it rain: their valiant temper
Men lose when they incline to treachery,
And then they fight like compell'd bears, would fly
Were they not tied.

ARCITE.   Kinsman, you might as well
Speak this and act it in your glass as to 70
His ear which now disdains you.

PALAMON.   Come up to me,
Quit me of these cold gyves, give me a sword,
Though it be rusty, and the charity
Of one meal lend me. Come before me then,
A good sword in thy hand, and do but say 75
That Emily is thine—I will forgive
The trespass thou hast done me, yea, my life,
If then thou carry't; and brave souls in shades
That have died manly, which will seek of me
Some news from earth, they shall get none but this— 80
That thou art brave and noble.

ARCITE.   Be content,
Again betake you to your hawthorn house.
With counsel of the night I will be here
With wholesome viands. These impediments
Will I file off; you shall have garments and 85
Perfumes to kill the smell o'th' prison. After,
When you shall stretch yourself and say but "Arcite,
I am in plight," there shall be at your choice
Both sword and armor.

PALAMON.   O you heavens, dares any
So noble bear a guilty business! None 90

---

68. *would*] who would; cf. *Macbeth*, V.vii.1.
70. *in your glass*] to your mirror.
72. *Quit*] free.
72. *gyves*] fetters.
78. *carry't*] win it.
78. *shades*] the underworld.
82. *betake you*] go into.
83. *counsel*] secrecy.
84. *viands*] food.
88. *in plight*] ready.

But only Arcite, therefore none but Arcite
In this kind is so bold.

ARCITE.   Sweet Palamon.

PALAMON.

I do embrace you, and your offer: for
Your offer do't I only, sir; your person,
Without hypocrisy, I may not wish   95
More than my sword's edge on't.

Wind horns off.

ARCITE.   You hear the horns.
Enter your muset lest this match between's
Be cross'd ere met. Give me your hand, farewell.
I'll bring you every needful thing: I pray you
Take comfort and be strong.

PALAMON.   Pray hold your promise,   100
And do the deed with a bent brow. Most certain
You love me not: be rough with me and pour
This oil out of your language. By this air,
I could for each word give a cuff, my stomach
Not reconcil'd by reason.

ARCITE.   Plainly spoken,   105
Yet pardon me hard language: when I spur
My horse, I chide him not; content and anger
In me have but one face. (*Wind horns.*)   Hark sir, they call
The scatter'd to the banquet; you must guess
I have an office there.

PALAMON.   Sir, your attendance   110
Cannot please heaven and I know your office

96.S.D.] *Q prints after l. 95.*   97. muset] *Dyce; Musicke Q.*
96.S.D. *off.*] *Bertram; of Cornets. Q.*   108.S.D.] *Q prints after l. 106.*

92. *kind*] manner.
96.S.D. *Wind*] sound.
97. *muset*] obsolete form of *meuse*, the "form" or nest of a hare.
98. *cross'd*] prevented.
101. *bent brow*] scowl.
103. *oil*] pretended courtesy.
104–105. *my . . . Not*] If my anger were not.
106. *pardon . . . language*] excuse me from speaking harshly.
110. *office*] duty.

Unjustly is achiev'd.

ARCITE.   I've a good title.
I am persuaded this question, sick between's,
By bleeding must be cur'd. I am a suitor
That to your sword you will bequeath this plea   115
And talk of it no more.

PALAMON.   But this one word.
You are going now to gaze upon my mistress—
For note you, mine she is—

ARCITE.   Nay then—

PALAMON.   Nay pray you.
You talk of feeding me to breed me strength:
You are going now to look upon a sun   120
That strengthens what it looks on; there you have
A vantage o'er me, but enjoy it till
I may enforce my remedy. Farewell.   *Exeunt.*

[III.ii]   *Enter* Jailer's Daughter *alone.*

DAUGHTER.
He has mistook the brake I meant, is gone
After his fancy. 'Tis now well-nigh morning.
No matter: would it were perpetual night
And darkness lord o'th' world. Hark, 'tis a wolf!
In me hath grief slain fear and, but for one thing,   5
I care for nothing, and that's Palamon.
I reck not if the wolves would jaw me, so
He had this file. What if I hallow'd for him?

112. I've] *1750;* If *Q.*   [III.ii]
119. strength:] *Colman; no punct. in*   1. mistook] *1750;* mistooke; *Q.*
Q.   1. brake] *1750 conj.;* Beake *Q.*
121.] *line ends there Q.*   7. reck] *1750;* wreake *Q.*
122. enjoy it] *Colman;* enjoy't *Q.*

112. *I've . . . title*] I have a perfect right to it.
113. *question*] dispute.
114. *I . . . suitor*] I beg you.
115. *plea*] lawsuit.
[III.ii]
  1. *brake*] thicket.
  7. *reck*] care.
  8. *hallow'd*] shouted.

I cannot hallow. If I whoop'd, what then?
If he not answer'd, I should call a wolf   10
And do him but that service. I have heard
Strange howls this livelong night: why may't not be
They have made prey of him? He has no weapons;
He cannot run; the jingling of his gyves
Might call fell things to listen, who have in them   15
A sense to know a man unarm'd and can
Smell where resistance is. I'll set it down
He's torn to pieces; they howl'd many together
And then they fed on him. So much for that;
Be bold to ring the bell. How stand I then?   20
All's char'd when he is gone. No, no, I lie;
My father's to be hang'd for his escape,
Myself to beg, if I priz'd life so much
As to deny my act, but that I would not,
Should I try death by dozens. I am mop'd: 25
Food took I none these two days, sipp'd some water.
I have not clos'd mine eyes
Save when my lids scour'd off their brine. Alas,
Dissolve, my life; let not my sense unsettle,
Lest I should drown, or stab, or hang myself.   30
O state of nature, fail together in me,
Since thy best props are warp'd! So, which way now?
The best way is the next way to a grave;
Each errant step beside is torment. Lo,
The moon is down, the crickets chirp, the screech owl   35

19. fed] *F;* feed *Q.*   28. brine] *1711;* bine *Q.*
26–27.] *Q lines end:* days/eyes.

---

14. *gyves*] fetters.
15. *fell*] fierce.
17. *set it down*] make a record of it; cf. *Hamlet,* I.v.106.
20. *bell*] the passing bell, rung to announce a death.
20. *How . . . then?*] cf. *Hamlet,* IV.iv.56.
21. *char'd*] done.
25. *mop'd*] bewildered.
28. *brine*] tears.
29. *sense*] reason.
33. *next*] nearest.
34. *errant*] wandering.
35. *The . . . down*] cf. *Macbeth,* II.i.2.

Calls in the dawn. All offices are done
Save what I fail in: but the point is this,
An end, and that is all.   *Exit.*

[III.iii]   *Enter* Arcite, *with meat, wine, and files* [*etc.*].

ARCITE.

I should be near the place. Ho! Cousin Palamon!

Enter Palamon.

PALAMON.

Arcite.

ARCITE.   The same. I have brought you food and files.
Come forth and fear not, here's no Theseus.

PALAMON.

Nor none so honest, Arcite.

ARCITE.   That's no matter,
We'll argue that hereafter. Come, take courage;   5
You shall not die thus beastly. Here, sir, drink;
I know you are faint; then I'll talk further with you.

PALAMON.

Arcite, thou might'st now poison me.

ARCITE.   I might:
But I must fear you first. Sit down, and good now,
No more of these vain parleys: let us not,   10
Having our ancient reputation with us,
Make talk for fools and cowards. To your health, sir!

PALAMON.

Do.

ARCITE. Pray sit down, then, and let me entreat you,
By all the honesty and honor in you,
No mention of this woman, 'twill disturb us.   15
We shall have time enough.

PALAMON.   Well, sir, I'll pledge you.

ARCITE.

Drink a good hearty draught, it breeds good blood, man.

12. sir] *this edn.;* &c *Q.*

36. *offices*] businesses.
[III.iii]
  0.1. *meat*] food.
  6. *beastly*] like an animal.
  17. *Drink . . . blood*] Tilley, W 461 "Good wine makes good blood."

Do not you feel it thaw you?

PALAMON.   Stay, I'll tell you
After a draught or two more.

ARCITE.   Spare it not,
The duke has more, coz. Eat now.

PALAMON.   Yes.

ARCITE.   I am glad   20
You have so good a stomach.

PALAMON.   I am gladder
I have so good meat to't.

ARCITE.   Is't not mad lodging,
Here in the wild woods, cousin?

PALAMON.   Yes, for them
That have wild consciences.

ARCITE.   How tastes your victuals?
Your hunger needs no sauce, I see.

PALAMON.   Not much.   25
But if it did, yours is too tart, sweet cousin.
What is this?

ARCITE.   Venison.

PALAMON.   'Tis a lusty meat.
Give me more wine: here, Arcite, to the wenches
We have known in our days. The lord steward's daughter!
Do you remember her?

ARCITE.   After you, coz.   30

PALAMON.
She lov'd a black-hair'd man.

ARCITE.   She did so: well, sir.

PALAMON.
And I have heard some call him Arcite, and—

ARCITE.
Out with't, faith.

PALAMON.   She met him in an arbor.
What did she there, coz? Play o'th' virginals?

18–27. *Stay . . . meat*] *prose in* Q.   23. them] *F; then* Q.

25.] "Hunger is the best sauce," Tilley, H 819.

28–41.] Littledale emphasizes the incongruity of Palamon's speeches in this scene with the sentiments he professes at V.i.98–107; see Introduction p. xix.

34. *virginals*] keyboard instruments.

ARCITE.

Something she did, sir.

PALAMON.   Made her groan a month for't: 35
Or two, or three, or ten.

ARCITE.   The marshal's sister
Had her share too, as I remember, cousin,
Else there be tales abroad. You'll pledge her?

PALAMON.   Yes.

ARCITE.

A pretty brown wench 'tis. There was a time
When young men went a-hunting, and a wood,   40
And a broad beech; and thereby hangs a tale—
Heigh-ho!

PALAMON.   For Emily, upon my life! Fool,
Away with this strain'd mirth. I say again,
That sigh was breath'd for Emily. Base cousin,
Dar'st thou break first?

ARCITE.   You are wide.

PALAMON.   By heaven and earth,   45
There's nothing in thee honest

ARCITE.   Then I'll leave you:
You are a beast now.

PALAMON.   As thou mak'st me, traitor.

ARCITE.

There's all things needful; files, and shirts, and perfumes.
I'll come again some two hours hence and bring
That that shall quiet all.

PALAMON.   A sword and armor.   50

ARCITE.

Fear me not. You are now too foul. Farewell.
Get off your trinkets: you shall want nought.

PALAMON.   Sirrah—

ARCITE.

I'll hear no more.   *Exit.*

PALAMON.   If he keep touch, he dies for't.   *Exit.*

35–36.] *Q lines end:* sir/ten/sister.   45–47. *By . . . traitor*] *prose in Q.*
41.] *Q line ends:* heigh-ho.

43. *strain'd*] forced.
51. *foul*] dirty.
53. *keep touch*] keeps his word.

[III.iv]   *Enter* Jailer's Daughter.
DAUGHTER.

    I am very cold, and all the stars are out too,
    The little stars and all, that look like aglets:
    The sun has seen my folly. Palamon!
    Alas, no; he's in heaven. Where am I now?
    Yonder's the sea, and there's a ship; how't tumbles!   5
    And there's a rock lies watching under water;
    Now, now, it beats upon it; now, now, now,
    There's a leak sprung, a sound one; how they cry!
    Run her before the wind, you'll lose all else:
    Up with a course or two and tack about, boys.   10
    Good night, good night, y'are gone. I am very hungry,
    Would I could find a fine frog: he would tell me
    News from all parts o'th' world, then would I make
    A carrack of a cockle shell, and sail
    By east and northeast to the King of Pygmies,   15
    For he tells fortunes rarely. Now my father,
    Twenty to one, is truss'd up in a trice
    Tomorrow morning. I'll say never a word.   *Sing.*

    For I'll cut my green coat, a foot above my knee,
    And I'll clip my yellow locks, an inch below mine eye,   20
              Hey nonny, nonny, nonny,
    He s' buy me a white cut, forth for to ride,
    And I'll go seek him, through the world that is so wide,
              Hey nonny, nonny, nonny.

    O for a prick now, like a nightingale,   25
    To put my breast against. I shall sleep like a top else.   *Exit.*

9. Run] *Skeat;* Vpon Q.   25–26.] *Q lines end:* breast/else.
10. tack] *F;* take *Q.*

---

    2. *aglets*] metal tags on laces.
    8. *sound*] large.
    10. *course*] a sail attached to the lower yards of a ship.
    14. *carrack*] a large cargo ship.
    19–20.] The first two lines of this song are related to the ballad of *Childe Waters*; Child, 63A.
    22. *s' buy*] shall buy.
    22. *cut*] cut-tail horse or gelding.
    25. *prick*] thorn; the nightingale was proverbially supposed to sit with its breast against a thorn to prevent itself from sleeping; Tilley, N 183.
    26. *sleep . . . top*] sleep soundly; Tilley, T 440.

[III.v]

Enter [Gerrold,] *a schoolmaster: four* Countrymen *and* [*one dressed as a*]
Bavian: *five* Wenches, *with a* Taborer.

GERROLD.

    Fie, fie, what tediosity and disinsanity
    Is here among ye! Have my rudiments
    Been labor'd so long with ye? milk'd unto ye?
    And, by a figure, even the very plum-broth
    And marrow of my understanding laid upon ye?   5
    And do you still cry "Where?" and "How?" and "Wherefore?"
    You most coarse frieze capacities, ye jean judgments,
    Have I said "Thus let be," and "There let be,"
    And "Then let be," and no man understand me?
    Proh deum, medius fidius, ye are all dunces.   10
    For why? Here stand I; here the duke comes; there are you,
    Close in the thicket. The duke appears; I meet him
    And unto him I utter learned things
    And many figures; he hears, and nods, and hums,
    And then cries "Rare!" and I go forward; at length   15
    I fling my cap up, mark there; then do you,
    As once did Meleager and the boar,
    Break comely out before him, like true lovers,
    Cast yourselves in a body decently,

III.v.] Scaena 6. *Q.*   1–20.] *arranged as prose in Q.*
0.2. Bavian] *1750; Baum. Q.*   7. jean] *Dyce;* jave *Q.*
0.2. *five*] *Dyce;* 2. *or* 3. *Q.*

  0.2. *Bavian*] baboon.
  0.2. *Taborer*] Morris-dancing is accompanied on the pipe and tabor,
a three-holed whistle and a small drum played simultaneously by one
player.
  1. *disinsanity*] madness; *dis-* is intensive.
  4. *by a figure*] metaphorically; Gerrold uses the phrase again at ll. 20,
103.
  4. *plum-broth*] cf. II.iii.70.
  7. *frieze*] coarse woolen cloth.
  7. *jean*] twilled cotton cloth.
  10. *Proh . . . fidius*] "O god, as true as heaven."
  12. *Close*] hidden.
  14. *figures*] figures of speech.
  14. *hums*] in appreciation.
  17. *Meleager*] see Ovid *Metamorphoses* viii. 260–424.
  19. *decently*] fittingly.

And sweetly, by a figure, trace and turn, boys.   20
FIRST COUNTRYMAN.
And sweetly we will do it, master Gerrold.
SECOND COUNTRYMAN.
Draw up the company. Where's the taborer?
THIRD COUNTRYMAN.
Why, Timothy!
TABORER.   Here, my mad boys; have at ye!
GERROLD.
But I say, where's these women?
FOURTH COUNTRYMAN.   Here's Friz and Maudline.
SECOND COUNTRYMAN.
And little Luce with the white legs, and bouncing Barbery. 25
FIRST COUNTRYMAN.
And freckled Nell, that never fail'd her master.
GERROLD.
Where be your ribands, maids? Swim with your bodies
And carry it sweetly and deliverly,
And now and then a favor and a frisk.
NELL.
Let us alone, sir.
GERROLD.   Where's the rest o'th' music?   30
THIRD COUNTRYMAN.
Dispers'd as you commanded.
GERROLD.   Couple, then,
And see what's wanting. Where's the bavian?
My friend, carry your tail without offense
Or scandal to the ladies; and be sure
You tumble with audacity and manhood,   35
And when you bark, do it with judgment.
BAVIAN.   Yes, sir.

24. these] *this edn.;* their *Q.*

---

20. *trace*] dance.
23. *mad*] wild.
25. *bouncing*] strapping.
28. *deliverly*] nimbly.
29. *favor*] attractive movement.
30. *Let us alone*] leave it to us.
35. *manhood*] courage.

GERROLD.

Quousque tandem? Here is a woman wanting.

FOURTH COUNTRYMAN.

We may go whistle: all the fat's i'th' fire.

GERROLD.

We have, as learned authors utter, wash'd a tile;

We have been *fatuus* and labored vainly.   40

SECOND COUNTRYMAN.

This is that scornful piece, that scurvy hilding

That gave her promise faithfully she would be here,

Cicely, the sempster's daughter:

The next gloves that I give her shall be dog-skin;

Nay, and she fail me once—you can tell, Arcas,   45

She swore by wine and bread she would not break.

GERROLD.

An eel and woman,

A learned poet says, unless by th' tail

And with thy teeth thou hold, will either fail:

In manners this was false position.   50

FIRST COUNTRYMAN.

A fire ill take her, does she flinch now?

THIRD COUNTRYMAN.   What

Shall we determine, sir?

GERROLD.   Nothing;

39.] *Q prints as two lines ending:*
have/tile.

---

37. *Quousque tandem*] "How long then?", indicating impatience; the opening words of Cicero's first speech against Catiline.

38. *We . . . fire*] Tilley, W 313: "You may whistle for it," you have no hope of success; F 79: "The fat is in the fire," everything is ruined.

39. *wash'd a tile*] Tilley, T 289, "To wash a tile," to labor in vain.

40. *fatuus*] "foolish."

41. *scurvy hilding*] wretched good-for-nothing.

44. *dog-skin*] poor quality leather; the best gloves were made of kidskin.

45. *and*] if.

46. *by . . . bread*] presumably the sacraments.

47–49. *An eel . . . fail*] the basis of these lines is proverbial; Tilley, W 640: "Who has a woman has an eel by the tail"; H 508: "As much hold of (i.e., reliance on) his word as of a wet eel by the tail."

50. *false position*] a false affirmation; perhaps with an allusion to the arithmetical "rule of false position."

51. *fire ill*] venereal disease.

51. *take*] infect.

Our business is become a nullity,
Yea, and a woeful and a piteous nullity.

FOURTH COUNTRYMAN.

Now, when the credit of our town lay on it,   55
Now to be frampold, now to piss o'th' nettle!
Go thy ways, I'll remember thee, I'll fit thee!

Enter Jailer's Daughter.

DAUGHTER [*sings*].

The George Alow came from the south,
From the coast of Barbary-a;
And there he met with brave gallants of war,   60
By one, by two, by three-a.

Well hail'd, well hail'd, you jolly gallants,
And whither now are you bound-a?
O let me have your company
Till I come to the sound-a.   65

There was three fools, fell out about an owlet:
The one said it was an owl,
The other he said nay,
The third he said it was a hawk, and her bells were cut away.

THIRD COUNTRYMAN.

There's a dainty madwoman, master,   70
Comes i'th' nick, as mad as a March hare:
If we can get her dance, we are made again:
I warrant her, she'll do the rarest gambols.

58.S.P.] *F; Q prints before l. 59.*   64–65.] *one line in Q.*
58.] *Q line ends: South, from.*   65. *I*] *1711; not in Q; we Weber.*
63–65.] *Q prints marginal S.D.:*   70–74.] *arranged as prose in Q.*
Chaire and stooles out.

---

56. *frampold*] peevish.
56. *piss o'th' nettle*] Tilley, N 132: "He has pissed on a nettle," he is in a bad temper.
57. *fit*] fix.
58–65.] A ballad of "the George Aloo and the Swifte-stake" was entered on the Stationers' Register, March 19, 1611; see Child, 285.
60. *gallants of war*] warships.
66–69.] This is the earliest extant version of a well-known nursery rhyme; see I. and P. Opie, eds., *The Oxford Dictionary of Nursery Rhymes* (Oxford, 1952), No. 525.
71. *i'th' nick*] at the right moment; Tilley, N 160.
71. *as . . . hare*] Tilley, H 148.

FIRST COUNTRYMAN.
  A mad woman? We are made, boys.
GERROLD.
  And are you mad, good woman?
DAUGHTER.   I would be sorry else.   75
  Give me your hand.
GERROLD.   Why?
DAUGHTER.   I can tell your fortune.
  You are a fool. Tell ten: I have pos'd him. Buzz!
  Friend, you must eat no white bread: if you do
  Your teeth will bleed extremely. Shall we dance, ho?
  I know you, y'are a tinker: sirrah tinker,   80
  Stop no more holes but what you should.
GERROLD.   *Dii boni,*
  A tinker, damsel?
DAUGHTER.   Or a conjurer:
  Raise me a devil now, and let him play
  Qui passa o'th' bells and bones.
GERROLD.   Go, take her,
  And fluently persuade her to a peace: 85
  Et opus exegi, quod nec Iovis ira, nec ignis—
  Strike up, and lead her in.
SECOND COUNTRYMAN.   Come, lass, let's trip it.
DAUGHTER.
  I'll lead.   *Wind horns.*
THIRD COUNTRYMAN. Do, do.

81–85.] *Q lines end:* should/ damsel/
play/ bones/ peace.

---

77. *Tell ten*] count your fingers, a test for a fool; Tilley, T 90a.

77. *pos'd*] puzzled.

78–79. *Friend . . . extremely*] These apparently nonsensical lines may contain an allusion to the popular belief that a man might suffer from sympathetic toothache during the pregnancy of his wife.

81. *Dii boni*] "good gods."

84. *Qui passa*] "who passed"; the name of a dance tune, *Chi passa per questa strada*; see Clement Robinson, *A Handefull of pleasant delites*, ed. H. E. Rollins (Cambridge, Mass., 1924), No. 21.

84. *bells and bones*] used to accompany dancing; here with punning reference to "bellibones," pretty girls.

86. *Et . . . ignis*] "And now my work is done, which neither the wrath of Jove, nor fire . . ."; Ovid *Metamorphoses* xv. 871, properly beginning "*Iamque opus . . ..*"

GERROLD.

 Persuasively and cunningly: away, boys,

 I hear the horns. Give me some meditation,   90

 And mark your cue.   *Exeunt all but* Gerrold.

    Pallas inspire me.

Enter Theseus, Pirithous, Hippolyta, Emilia, *Arcite, and train.*

THESEUS.

 This way the stag took.

GERROLD.   Stay, and edify.

THESEUS.*

 What have we here?

PIRITHOUS.   Some country sport, upon my life, sir.

THESEUS.

 Well, sir, go forward: we will edify.

 Ladies, sit down, we'll stay it.   95

GERROLD.

 Thou doughty duke, all hail! All hail, sweet ladies!

THESEUS.

 This is a cold beginning.

GERROLD.

 If you but favor, our country pastime made is.

 We are a few of those collected here,

 That ruder tongues distinguish "villager";   100

 And to say verity, and not to fable,

 We are a merry rout, or else a rable,

 Or company, or, by a figure, *choris,*

 That 'fore thy dignity will dance a morris.

 And I, that am the rectifier of all,   105

 By title *pedagogus,* that let fall

90–91.] *Q lines end:* some/ cue/ me. 94.S.P. THESEUS] *F; Per. Q.*
91.S.D.] *Q prints after l. 89.*

---

 91. *inspire*] trisyllabic.

 92. *edify*] be instructed.

 100. *distinguish*] call.

 102,103,116,119.] The Quarto spelling of the rhyme words is retained to emphasize Gerrold's strained rhyming.

 104. *morris*] a grotesque dance, performed in fancy costume; the name is derived from "morys", a variant form of the adjective "moorish."

 106. *pedagogus*] "schoolmaster."

The birch upon the breeches of the small ones,
And humble with a ferula the tall ones,
Do here present this machine, or this frame;
And dainty duke, whose doughty dismal fame   110
From Dis to Dedalus, from post to pillar,
Is blown abroad, help me, thy poor well-willer,
And, with thy twinkling eyes, look right and straight
Upon this mighty *Morr*—of mickle weight—
Is—now comes in, which, being glued together,   115
Makes *Morris*, and the cause that we came hether.
The body of our sport, of no small study,
I first appear, though rude, and raw, and muddy,
To speak, before thy noble grace, this tenner:
At whose great feet I offer up my penner.   120
The next, the Lord of May and Lady bright;
The Chambermaid and Servingman, by night
That seek out silent hanging; then mine Host
And his fat Spouse, that welcomes, to their cost,
The galled traveller, and with a beck'ning   125
Informs the tapster to inflame the reck'ning;
Then the beest eating Clown, and next, the Fool,

127. beest-eating] *Kökeritz;* beast
eating *Q*.

---

108. *ferula*] cane or flat ruler.
109. *machine*] contrivance; accented on the first syllable.
109. *frame*] device.
111. *Dis to Dedalus*] nonsense; *Dis*, Pluto, god of the underworld; *Dedalus*, Cretan inventor who built the labyrinth.
111. *from . . . pillar*] Tilley, P 328.
114–115. *Morr . . . Is*] Gerrold's riddle may depend on the meanings "Moor" and "ice" for the separate syllables of *morris*.
114. *mickle*] great.
117. *of . . . study*] carefully thought out.
119. *tenner*] i.e., "tenor," speech.
120. *penner*] pen-case.
121–129.] These figures appeared in Francis Beaumont's *Masque of the Inner Temple and Gray's Inn*; see Introduction pp. xii, xx.
123. *hanging*] curtain covering a wall or bed.
125. *galled*] sore.
127. *beest-eating*] Kökeritz explains that *beest* is the milk which a cow gives for the first few days after calving; in the south of England it was thought unfit for human consumption.
127. *Clown*] countryman.

The Bavian, with long tail and eke long tool,
Cum multis aliis that make a dance:
Say "ay," and all shall presently advance.   130

THESEUS.

Ay, ay, by any means, dear domine.

PIRITHOUS.

Produce.

Knock for [the] school.

GERROLD.

Intrate filii, come forth and foot it.

Enter the dance: music, dance.

Ladies, if we have been merry,
And have pleas'd ye with a derry,   135
And a derry and a down,
Say the schoolmaster's no clown:
Duke, if we have pleas'd thee too,
And have done as good boys should do,
Give us but a tree or twain   140
For a maypole, and again,
Ere another year run out,
We'll make thee laugh, and all this rout.

THESEUS.

Take twenty, domine. How does my sweetheart?

HIPPOLYTA.

Never so pleas'd, sir.

EMILIA.   'Twas an excellent dance,   145
And for a preface, I never heard a better.

132.1, 133.1. *Knock . . . the dance:*]
Q prints in margin.
133.S.P.   GERROLD]   *Colman;   not
in Q.*
133.1. *music, dance*]   *Q prints after
l. 132.*

134–143.] *italic in Q.*
135. ye] *1750; thee Q.*
138. thee] *F; three Q.*
145–146.] *Q lines end:* sir/ preface/
better.

---

128. *Bavian*] baboon.
129. *Cum multis aliis*] "with many others."   ,
130. *presently*] immediately.
131. *domine*] master.
132.1. *school*] The dancers are Gerrold's pupils.
133. *Intrate filii*] "come in, boys."

THESEUS.

Schoolmaster, I thank you. One see 'em all rewarded.

PIRITHOUS.

And here's something to paint your pole withal.

THESEUS.

Now to our sports again.

GERROLD.

May the stag thou hunt'st stand long,   150
And thy dogs be swift and strong:
May they kill him without lets,
And the ladies eat his dowsets.

Wind horns. [*Exeunt* Theseus, Pirithous, Hippolyta, Emilia, *Arcite and train.*]

Come, we are all made. *Dii deaeque omnes,*
Ye have danc'd rarely, wenches.   *Exeunt.* 155

[III.vi]   *Enter* Palamon *from the bush.*

PALAMON.

About this hour my cousin gave his faith
To visit me again, and with him bring
Two swords and two good armors; if he fail,
He's neither man nor soldier. When he left me,
I did not think a week could have restor'd   5
My lost strength to me, I was grown so low
And crest-fall'n with my wants. I thank thee, Arcite,
Thou art yet a fair foe, and I feel myself,
With this refreshing, able once again
To out-dure danger. To delay it longer   10
Would make the world think, when it comes to hearing,
That I lay fatting, like a swine, to fight,
And not a soldier: therefore this blest morning
Shall be the last; and that sword he refuses,

153.1. *Wind horns*] Q *prints after*   154–155.] Q *lines end:* made/ wen-
made.   ches.
                                        III.vi] Scaena 7. Q.

152. *lets*] hindrances.
153. *dowsets*] testicles.
154. *Dii deaeque omnes*] "all ye gods and goddesses."
[III.vi]
10. *out-dure*] outlast.

If it but hold, I kill him with; 'tis justice.   15
So, love and fortune for me!

Enter Arcite *with armors and swords.*

O, good morrow.

ARCITE.
Good morrow, noble kinsman.
PALAMON.   I have put you
To too much pains, sir.
ARCITE.   That too much, fair cousin,
Is but a debt to honor, and my duty.
PALAMON.
Would you were so in all, sir: I could wish ye   20
As kind a kinsman, as you force me find
A beneficial foe, that my embraces
Might thank ye, not my blows.
ARCITE.   I shall think either,
Well done, a noble recompense.
PALAMON.   Then I shall quit you.
ARCITE.
Defy me in these fair terms, and you show   25
More than a mistress to me: no more anger,
As you love anything that's honorable.
We were not bred to talk, man; when we are arm'd
And both upon our guards, then let our fury,
Like meeting of two tides, fly strongly from us;   30
And then to whom the birthright of this beauty
Truly pertains—without upbraidings, scorns,
Despisings of our persons and such poutings,
Fitter for girls and schoolboys—will be seen,
And quickly, yours or mine. Will't please you arm, sir?   35
Or, if you feel yourself not fitting yet
And furnish'd with your old strength, I'll stay, cousin,
And every day discourse you into health,
As I am spar'd. Your person I am friends with,
And I could wish I had not said I lov'd her,   40

16.S.D.] *Q prints after* morrow.

24. *quit*] repay.
37. *stay*] wait.
38. *discourse*] talk.

Though I had died; but loving such a lady,
And justifying my love, I must not fly from't.

PALAMON.

 Arcite, thou art so brave an enemy
 That no man but thy cousin's fit to kill thee.
 I am well and lusty: choose your arms.

ARCITE.   Choose you, sir. 45

PALAMON.

 Wilt thou exceed in all, or dost thou do it
 To make me spare thee?

ARCITE.   If you think so, cousin,
 You are deceived, for as I am a soldier,
 I will not spare you.

PALAMON.   That's well said.

ARCITE.   You'll find it.

PALAMON.

 Then, as I am an honest man, and love
 With all the justice of affection,
 I'll pay thee soundly. This I'll take. [*Chooses armor.*]

ARCITE.   That's mine, then.
 I'll arm you first.

PALAMON.   Do. Pray thee tell me, cousin,
 Where got'st thou this good armor?

ARCITE.   'Tis the duke's,
 And to say true, I stole it. Do I pinch you?

PALAMON.   No. 55

ARCITE.

 Is't not too heavy?

PALAMON.   I have worn a lighter,
 But I shall make it serve.

ARCITE.   I'll buckle't close.

PALAMON.

 By any means.

ARCITE.   You care not for a grand-guard?

PALAMON.

 No, no, we'll use no horses. I perceive

---

58. *grand-guard*] an extra plate of armor to protect the left shoulder and side in jousting.

You would fain be at that fight.

ARCITE.   I am indifferent.   60

PALAMON.

Faith, so am I. Good cousin, thrust the buckle
Through far enough.

ARCITE.   I warrant you.

PALAMON.   My casque now.

ARCITE.

Will you fight bare-arm'd?

PALAMON.   We shall be the nimbler.

ARCITE.

But use your gauntlets, though; those are o'th' least.
Prithee take mine, good cousin.

PALAMON.   Thank you, Arcite.   65

How do I look? Am I fall'n much away?

ARCITE.

Faith, very little; love has us'd you kindly.

PALAMON.

I'll warrant thee, I'll strike home.

ARCITE.   Do, and spare not:

I'll give you cause, sweet cousin.

PALAMON.   Now to you, sir.

Methinks this armor's very like that, Arcite,   70
Thou wor'st that day the three kings fell, but lighter.

ARCITE.

That was a very good one; and that day,
I well remember, you outdid me, cousin;
I never saw such valor. When you charg'd
Upon the left wing of the enemy,   75
I spurr'd hard to come up, and under me
I had a right good horse.

PALAMON.   You had indeed;

A bright bay, I remember.

ARCITE.   Yes. But all

Was vainly labor'd in me; you outwent me,
Nor could my wishes reach you; yet a little   80

---

60. *that fight*] i.e., on horseback.
62. *warrant*] promise.
62. *casque*] helmet.

I did by imitation.

PALAMON.   More by virtue;

You are modest, cousin.

ARCITE.   When I saw you charge first,

Methought I heard a dreadful clap of thunder

Break from the troop.

PALAMON.   But still before that flew

The lightning of your valor. Stay a little,   85

Is not this piece too strait?

ARCITE.   No, no, 'tis well.

PALAMON.

I would have nothing hurt thee but my sword,

A bruise would be dishonor.

ARCITE.   Now I am perfect.

PALAMON.

Stand off, then.

ARCITE.   Take my sword; I hold it better.

PALAMON.

I thank ye. No, keep it; your life lies on it.   90

Here's one, if it but hold, I ask no more

For all my hopes. My cause and honor guard me!

ARCITE.

And me my love!

They bow several ways, then advance and stand.

Is there aught else to say?

PALAMON.

This only, and no more. Thou art mine aunt's son,

And that blood we desire to shed is mutual;   95

In me, thine, and in thee, mine: my sword

Is in my hand, and if thou kill'st me,

The gods and I forgive thee. If there be

A place prepar'd for those that sleep in honor,

I wish his weary soul that falls may win it.   100

Fight bravely, cousin: give me thy noble hand.

93.S.D.] *Q prints in margin.*

---

86. *strait*] tight.

89. *hold it*] think it is.

93.S.D. *several*] different.

ARCITE.

    Here, Palamon. This hand shall never more
Come near thee with such friendship.

PALAMON.   I commend thee.

ARCITE.

    If I fall, curse me, and say I was a coward;
For none but such dare die in these just trials.   105
Once more farewell, my cousin.

PALAMON.   Farewell, Arcite.

Fight. Horns within; they stand.

ARCITE.

    Lo, cousin, lo, our folly has undone us.

PALAMON.   Why?

ARCITE.

    This is the duke a-hunting, as I told you:
If we be found, we are wretched. O, retire,
For honor's sake and safety, presently   110
Into your bush again. Sir, we shall find
Too many hours to die in; gentle cousin,
If you be seen, you perish instantly
For breaking prison, and I, if you reveal me,
For my contempt: then all the world will scorn us,   115
And say we had a noble difference,
But base disposers of it.

PALAMON.   No, no, cousin,
I will no more be hidden, nor put off
This great adventure to a second trial.
I know your cunning and I know your cause: 120
He that faints now, shame take him! Put thyself
Upon thy present guard—

ARCITE.   You are not mad?

PALAMON.

    Or I will make th'advantage of this hour

110. safety] *1750;* safely Q.   112. in; gentle cousin,] *Colman;* in,
                                  gentle Cosen: Q.

106.1. *stand*] stop.
110. *presently*] immediately.
116. *difference*] quarrel.
117. *disposers*] managers.

Mine own, and what to come shall threaten me
I fear less than my fortune. Know, weak cousin,   125
I love Emilia, and in that I'll bury
Thee and all crosses else.

ARCITE.   Then come what can come,
Thou shalt know, Palamon, I dare as well
Die as discourse or sleep: only this fears me,
The law will have the honor of our ends.   130
Have at thy life!

PALAMON.   Look to thine own well, Arcite!

Fight again. Horns. Enter Theseus, Hippolyta, Emilia, Pirithous, *and*
train.

THESEUS.
What ignorant and mad malicious traitors
Are you, that 'gainst the tenor of my laws
Are making battle, thus like knights appointed,
Without my leave and officers of arms?   135
By Castor, both shall die.

PALAMON.   Hold thy word, Theseus:
We are certainly both traitors, both despisers
Of thee and of thy goodness. I am Palamon,
That cannot love thee, he that broke thy prison—
Think well what that deserves—and this is Arcite.   140
A bolder traitor never trod thy ground,
A falser ne'er seem'd friend; this is the man
Was begg'd and banish'd; this is he contemns thee
And what thou dar'st do, and in this disguise,
Against thy own edict, follows thy sister,   145
That fortunate bright star, the fair Emilia;
Whose servant—if there be a right in seeing
And first bequeathing of the soul to—justly
I am; and, which is more, dares think her his.
This treachery, like a most trusty lover,   150

140. Arcite.] *Colman; no punct. in* Q.   145. thy own] *Dyce;* this owne Q.

127. *crosses*] obstacles.
127. *come . . . come*] cf. II.iii.17.
134. *appointed*] armed.
136. *By Castor*] "In old writings Roman women do not swear by Hercules,
nor men by Castor" (Aulus Gellius, cited in C. H. Herford and P. Simpson,
Ben Jonson [Oxford, 1932], iv.336–337.)

I call'd him now to answer. If thou be'st
As thou art spoken, great and virtuous,
The true decider of all injuries,
Say "Fight again" and thou shalt see me, Theseus,
Do such a justice, thou thyself wilt envy.   155
Then take my life: I'll woo thee to't.
PIRITHOUS.   O heaven,
What more than man is this!
THESEUS.   I have sworn.
ARCITE.   We seek not
Thy breath of mercy, Theseus: 'tis to me
A thing as soon to die, as thee to say it,
And no more mov'd. Where this man calls me traitor,   160
Let me say thus much: if in love be treason,
In service of so excellent a beauty,
As I love most, and in that faith will perish,
As I have brought my life here to confirm it,
As I have serv'd her truest, worthiest,   165
As I dare kill this cousin that denies it,
So let me be most traitor and ye please me.
For scorning thy edict, duke, ask that lady
Why she is fair and why her eyes command me
Stay here to love her, and if she say "traitor,"   170
I am a villain fit to lie unburied.
PALAMON.
Thou shalt have pity of us both, O Theseus,
If unto neither thou show mercy. Stop,
As thou art just, thy noble ear against us;
As thou art valiant, for thy cousin's soul,   175
Whose twelve strong labors crown his memory,
Let's die together, at one instant, duke.
Only a little let him fall before me,
That I may tell my soul he shall not have her.
THESEUS.
I grant your wish; for, to say true, your cousin   180
Has ten times more offended, for I gave him
More mercy than you found, sir, your offences

175. valiant,] *Colman;* valiant; *Q.*

---

175. *thy cousin*] Hercules; cf. I.i.66, II.v.2, V.iii.119.

Being no more than his. None here speak for 'em,
For ere the sun set both shall sleep forever.

HIPPOLYTA.

 Alas the pity! Now or never, sister,   185
 Speak, not to be denied. That face of yours
 Will bear the curses else of after ages
 For these lost cousins.

EMILIA.   In my face, dear sister,
 I find no anger to 'em, nor no ruin;
 The misadventure of their own eyes kill 'em: 190
 Yet that I will be woman and have pity,
 My knees shall grow to th' ground, but I'll get mercy.
 Help me, dear sister; in a deed so virtuous
 The powers of all women will be with us.
 Most royal brother—

HIPPOLYTA.   Sir, by our tie of marriage—   195

EMILIA.

 By your own spotless honor—

HIPPOLYTA.   By that faith,
 That fair hand and that honest heart you gave me—

EMILIA.

 By that you would have pity in another,
 By your own virtues infinite—

HIPPOLYTA.   By valor,
 By all the chaste nights I have ever pleas'd you—   200

THESEUS.

 These are strange conjurings.

PIRITHOUS.   Nay, then, I'll in too.—
 By all our friendship, sir, by all our dangers,
 By all you love most, wars, and this sweet lady—

EMILIA.

 By that you would have trembled to deny
 A blushing maid—

HIPPOLYTA.   By your own eyes, by strength,   205

201–202. Nay . . . dangers] *one line
in Q.*

---

198. *By . . . another*] by the pity you would wish anyone else to show.
 201. *conjurings*] entreaties.
 204–205. *By . . . maid*] by your obligation to attend to the pleas of maidens in distress; but cf. ll. 230–235, where Emilia reminds Theseus of a particular promise.

In which you swore I went beyond all women,
Almost all men, and yet I yielded, Theseus—

PIRITHOUS.

To crown all this; by your most noble soul,
Which cannot want due mercy, I beg first—

HIPPOLYTA.

Next hear my prayers—

EMILIA.   Last let me entreat, sir—   210

PIRITHOUS.

For mercy.

HIPPOLYTA.   Mercy.

EMILIA.   Mercy on these princes.

THESEUS.

Ye make my faith reel. Say I felt
Compassion to 'em both, how would you place it?

EMILIA.

Upon their lives; but with their banishments.

THESEUS.

You are a right woman, sister; you have pity,   215
But want the understanding where to use it.
If you desire their lives, invent a way
Safer than banishment: can these two live
And have the agony of love about 'em,
And not kill one another? Every day   220
They'd fight about you; hourly bring your honor
In public question with their swords. Be wise, then,
And here forget 'em; it concerns your credit
And my oath equally. I have said they die:
Better they fall by th' law than one another.   225
Bow not my honor.

EMILIA.   O my noble brother,
That oath was rashly made and in your anger;
Your reason will not hold it. If such vows
Stand for express will, all the world must perish.
Beside, I have another oath 'gainst yours,   230
Of more authority, I am sure more love;
Not made in passion neither, but good heed.

226. *Bow*] bend.   232. *passion*] anger.
229. *express*] fixed.

THESEUS.
    What is it, sister?
PIRITHOUS.   Urge it home, brave lady.
EMILIA.
    That you would ne'er deny me any thing
    Fit for my modest suit and your free granting.   235
    I tie you to your word now; if ye fall in't,
    Think how you maim your honor—
    For now I am set a-begging, sir, I am deaf
    To all but your compassion—how their lives
    Might breed the ruin of my name, opinion.   240
    Shall any thing that loves me perish for me?
    That were a cruel wisdom: do men prune
    The straight young boughs that blush with thousand blossoms,
    Because they may be rotten? O Duke Theseus,
    The goodly mothers that have groan'd for these,   245
    And all the longing maids that ever lov'd,
    If your vow stand, shall curse me and my beauty,
    And in their funeral songs for these two cousins
    Despise my cruelty and cry woe worth me,
    Till I am nothing but the scorn of women.   250
    For heaven's sake, save their lives and banish 'em.
THESEUS.
    On what conditions?
EMILIA.   Swear 'em never more
    To make me their contention, or to know me,
    To tread upon thy dukedom; and to be,
    Wherever they shall travel, ever strangers   255
    To one another.
PALAMON.   I'll be cut a-pieces
    Before I take this oath: forget I love her?
    O all ye gods despise me, then. Thy banishment
    I not mislike, so we may fairly carry
    Our swords and cause along; else, never trifle,   260

---

240. name, opinion.] *Colman;*   255–256. Wherever . . . another]
name; Opinion, *Q*.   *one line in Q.*

---

236. *fall*] fail.
240. *opinion*] consider.
249. *woe worth me*] woe betide me.

But take our lives, duke. I must love, and will:
And for that love must and dare kill this cousin,
On any piece the earth has.
THESEUS.   Will you, Arcite,
Take these conditions?
PALAMON.   He's a villain, then.
PIRITHOUS.
These are men!   265
ARCITE.
No, never, duke; 'tis worse to me than begging,
To take my life so basely. Though I think
I never shall enjoy her, yet I'll preserve
The honor of affection and die for her,
Make death a devil.   270
THESEUS.
What may be done? For now I feel compassion.
PIRITHOUS.
Let it not fall again, sir.
THESEUS.   Say, Emilia,
If one of them were dead, as one must, are you
Content to take the other to your husband?
They cannot both enjoy you. They are princes   275
As goodly as your own eyes, and as noble
As ever fame yet spoke of; look upon 'em,
And, if you can love, end this difference.
I give consent. Are you content too, princes?
BOTH.
With all our souls.
THESEUS.   He that she refuses   280
Must die, then.
BOTH.   Any death thou canst invent, duke.
PALAMON.
If I fall from that mouth, I fall with favor,
And lovers yet unborn shall bless my ashes.
ARCITE.
If she refuse me, yet my grave will wed me,

274. the other] *1750;* th'other *Q.*

---

270. *Make*] though you make.

And soldiers sing my epitaph.

THESEUS.   Make choice, then.   285

EMILIA.

   I cannot, sir; they are both too excellent:

   For me, a hair shall never fall of these men.

HIPPOLYTA.

   What will become of 'em?

THESEUS.   Thus I ordain it;

   And, by mine honor, once again, it stands,

   Or both shall die. You shall both to your country,   290

   And each, within this month, accompanied

   With three fair knights, appear again in this place,

   In which I'll plant a pyramid; and whether,

   Before us that are here, can force his cousin

   By fair and knightly strength to touch the pillar,   295

   He shall enjoy her; the other lose his head,

   And all his friends; nor shall he grudge to fall,

   Nor think he dies with interest in this lady.

   Will this content ye?

PALAMON.   Yes. Here, cousin Arcite,

   I am friends again, till that hour.

ARCITE.   I embrace ye.   300

THESEUS.

   Are you content, sister?

EMILIA.   Yes, I must, sir,

   Else both miscarry.

THESEUS.   Come, shake hands again, then,

   And take heed, as you are gentlemen, this quarrel

   Sleep till the hour prefix'd, and hold your course.

PALAMON.

   We dare not fail thee, Theseus.

THESEUS.   Come, I'll give ye   305

   Now usage like to princes and to friends.

   When ye return, who wins I'll settle here,

   Who loses, yet I'll weep upon his bier.   *Exeunt.*

286. excellent:] *1711; no punct. in Q.*

_____

293. *whether*] whichever.

302. *miscarry*] perish.

307. *here*] in my heart, in my friendship.

[IV.i]   *Enter* Jailer *and his* Friend.

JAILER.

> Hear you no more? Was nothing said of me
> Concerning the escape of Palamon?
> Good sir, remember.

FIRST FRIEND.   Nothing that I heard,

> For I came home before the business
> Was fully ended. Yet I might perceive,   5
> Ere I departed, a great likelihood
> Of both their pardons; for Hippolyta
> And fair-eyed Emily upon their knees
> Begg'd with such handsome pity, that the duke,
> Methought, stood staggering, whether he should follow   10
> His rash oath or the sweet compassion
> Of those two ladies; and to second them
> That truly noble prince, Pirithous,
> Half his own heart, set in too, that I hope
> All shall be well: neither heard I one question   15
> Of your name or his 'scape.

JAILER.   Pray heaven it hold so!

                    Enter Second Friend.

SECOND FRIEND.

> Be of good comfort, man; I bring you news,
> Good news.

JAILER.   They are welcome.

SECOND FRIEND.   Palamon has clear'd you

> And got your pardon, and discover'd how
> And by whose means he escap'd, which was your
>   daughter's,   20
> Whose pardon is procur'd too; and the prisoner,
> Not to be held ungrateful to her goodness,
> Has given a sum of money to her marriage,
> A large one, I'll assure you.

JAILER.   Ye are a good man

16.1.] Q *prints after* 'scape.   19.] Q *line ends:* discover'd.

10. *staggering*] wavering.
16. *'scape*] escape.
21–24.] At V.iv.31–32 Palamon gives the Jailer his purse towards his
daughter's dowry; cf. II.i.1–10.

And ever bring good news.

FIRST FRIEND.   How was it ended?   25

SECOND FRIEND.

Why, as it should be; they that never begg'd
But they prevail'd, had their suits fairly granted:
The prisoners have their lives.

FIRST FRIEND.   I knew 'twould be so.

SECOND FRIEND.

But there be new conditions, which you'll hear of
At better time.

JAILER.   I hope they are good.

SECOND FRIEND.   They arc honorable: 30

How good they'll prove, I know not.

FIRST FRIEND.   'Twill be known.

Enter Wooer.

WOOER.

Alas, sir, where's your daughter?

JAILER.   Why do you ask?

WOOER.

O sir, when did you see her?

SECOND FRIEND.   How he looks!

JAILER.

This morning.

WOOER.   Was she well? Was she in health, sir?
When did she sleep?

FIRST FRIEND.   These are strange questions.   35

JAILER.

I do not think she was very well; for now
You make me mind her, but this very day
I ask'd her questions and she answered me
So far from what she was, so childishly,
So sillily, as if she were a fool,   40
An innocent, and I was very angry.
But what of her, sir?

WOOER.   Nothing but my pity:
But you must know it, and as good by me

26. never] *1750;* nev'r *Q.*   *line in Q.*
31.1.] *Q prints after* know not.   42–43. Nothing . . . me] *one line in*
34–35. *Was she well . . . sleep?*] *one*   *Q.*

−87−

As by another that less loves her—
JAILER.
    Well, sir?
FIRST FRIEND. Not right?
SECOND FRIEND.   Not well?
WOOER.   No, sir, not well: 45
    'Tis too true, she is mad.
FIRST FRIEND.   It cannot be.
WOOER.
    Believe, you'll find it so.
JAILER.   I half suspected
    What you told me: the gods comfort her!
    Either this was her love to Palamon,
    Or fear of my miscarrying on his 'scape,   50
    Or both.
WOOER.   'Tis likely.
JAILER.   But why all this haste, sir?
WOOER.
    I'll tell you quickly. As I late was angling
    In the great lake that lies behind the palace,
    From the far shore, thick set with reeds and sedges,
    As patiently I was attending sport,   55
    I heard a voice, a shrill one, and attentive
    I gave my ear, when I might well perceive
    'Twas one that sung, and by the smallness of it
    A boy or woman. I then left my angle
    To his own skill, came near, but yet perceiv'd not   60
    Who made the sound, the rushes and the reeds
    Had so encompass'd it. I laid me down
    And listen'd to the words she sung, for then,
    Through a small glade cut by the fishermen,
    I saw it was your daughter.
JAILER.   Pray go on, sir.   65

46.] Q prints S.P. "Woo." before this   63. sung] F; song Q.
line.

---

55. attending sport] concentrating on my fishing.
58. smallness] softness.
59. angle] fishing tackle.
64. glade] passage.

WOOER.

 She sung much, but no sense; only I heard her
 Repeat this often: "Palamon is gone,
 Is gone to th' wood to gather mulberries;
 I'll find him out tomorrow."

FIRST FRIEND.   Pretty soul!

WOOER.

 "His shackles will betray him, he'll be taken,   70
 And what shall I do then? I'll bring a bevy,
 A hundred black-eyed maids that love as I do,
 With chaplets on their heads of daffadillies,
 With cherry lips and cheeks of damask roses,
 And all we'll dance an antic 'fore the duke   75
 And beg his pardon." Then she talk'd of you, sir;
 That you must lose your head tomorrow morning,
 And she must gather flowers to bury you,
 And see the house made handsome. Then she sung
 Nothing but "Willow, willow, willow," and between 80
 Ever was "Palamon, fair Palamon,"
 And "Palamon was a tall young man." The place
 Was knee-deep where she sat; her careless tresses
 A wreath of bullrush rounded; about her stuck
 Thousand fresh water flowers of several colors; 85
 That methought she appear'd like the fair nymph
 That feeds the lake with waters, or as Iris
 Newly dropp'd down from heaven. Rings she made
 Of rushes that grew by, and to 'em spoke
 The prettiest posies: "Thus our true love's tied," 90

84. wreath] *1750;* wreake *Q.*

---

71. *bevy*] company.
73. *chaplets*] garlands.
74. *damask*] deep pink or light red.
75. *antic*] alluding to her participation in the morris in III.v.
80. *Willow*] refrain of a song best known from the adaptation in *Othello,*
IV.iii; Chappell, 207.
82. *tall*] brave, handsome.
83. *knee-deep*] with rushes; see l. 61.
87. *Iris*] messenger of Juno; goddess of the rainbow.
88–89. *Rings . . . rushes*] Rush-rings were used by country people as
keepsakes or wedding rings.
90. *posies*] mottoes inscribed on rings.

"This you may lose, not me," and many a one;
And then she wept, and sung again, and sigh'd,
And with the same breath smil'd and kiss'd her hand.

SECOND FRIEND.

Alas, what pity it is !

WOOER.   I made in to her:
She saw me and straight sought the flood; I sav'd her   95
And set her safe to land; when presently
She slipp'd away and to the city made,
With such a cry and swiftness that, believe me,
She left me far behind her. Three or four
I saw from far off cross her; one of 'em   100
I knew to be your brother; where she stayed and fell,
Scarce to be got away. I left them with her,
And hither came to tell you.

    Enter [Jailer's] Brother, [Jailer's] Daughter *and others.*

                     Here they are.

DAUGHTER [*sings*].
May you never more enjoy the light, etc.
Is not this a fine song?

BROTHER.   O, a very fine one.   105

DAUGHTER.

I can sing twenty more.

BROTHER.   I think you can.

DAUGHTER.

Yes truly can I. I can sing *The Broom,*
And *Bonny Robin.* Are not you a tailor?

BROTHER.

Yes.

DAUGHTER. Where's my wedding gown?

BROTHER.   I'll bring it tomorrow.

DAUGHTER.

Do, very early; I must be abroad else,   110

101.] *Q line ends:* stayed.   110. early] *1750;* rarely *Q.*
103.S.D.] *Q prints after l. 102.*

---

    100. *cross*] meet.
    104. *May . . . light*] The song in which this line occurs has not been identified.
    107. *The Broom*] popular song first mentioned in 1559; Chappell, 459.
    108. *Bonny Robin*] a song of which Ophelia sings a snatch in her madness, *Hamlet,* IV.v.187; Chappell, 234.

To call the maids and pay the minstrels;
For I must lose my maidenhead by cocklight,
'Twill never thrive else.   *Sings.*
    O fair, O sweet, etc.
BROTHER.
    You must e'en take it patiently.
JAILER.   'Tis true.   115
DAUGHTER.
    Good e'en, good men. Pray, did you ever hear
    Of one young Palamon?
JAILER.   Yes, wench, we know him.
DAUGHTER.
    Is't not a fine young gentleman?
JAILER.   'Tis, love.
BROTHER.
    By no mean cross her, she is then distemper'd
    Far worse than now she shows.
FIRST FRIEND.   Yes, he's a fine man.   120
DAUGHTER.
    O, is he so? You have a sister.
FIRST FRIEND.   Yes.
DAUGHTER.
    But she shall never have him, tell her so,
    For a trick that I know. Y'had best look to her,
    For if she see him once, she's gone; she's done
    And undone in an hour. All the young maids   125
    Of our town are in love with him, but I laugh at 'em
    And let 'em all alone. Is't not a wise course?
FIRST FRIEND.   Yes.
DAUGHTER. There is at least two hundred now with child by him,
    There must be four; yet I keep close for all this,
    Close as a cockle; and all these must be boys—   130
    He has the trick on't—and at ten years old

113. S.D.] *Q prints after l. 114.*   120. Far] *1711;* For *Q.*

---

112. *by cocklight*] before dawn.
114. *O fair, O sweet*] song printed with Sidney's *Arcadia* (1598).
129. *close*] shut.
130. *Close as a cockle*] Tilley, C 499; *cockle* = clam.
131. *on't*] of it.

They must be all gelt for musicians
And sing the wars of Theseus.

SECOND FRIEND.   This is strange.

BROTHER.

As ever you heard: but say nothing.

FIRST FRIEND.   No.

DAUGHTER.

They come from all parts of the dukedom to him.   135
I'll warrant ye, he had not so few last night
As twenty to dispatch. He'll tickle't up
In two hours, if his hand be in.

JAILER.   She's lost

Past all cure!

BROTHER.   Heaven forbid, man!

DAUGHTER.

Come hither; you are a wise man.

FIRST FRIEND.   Does she know him?   140

SECOND FRIEND.

No, would she did!

DAUGHTER.   You are master of a ship?

JAILER.

Yes.

DAUGHTER. Where's your compass?

JAILER.   Here.

DAUGHTER.   Set it to th' north:
And now direct your course to th' wood, where Palamon
Lies longing for me. For the tackling,
Let me alone. Come, weigh, my hearts, cheerily all.   145
Owgh, owgh, owgh! 'Tis up; the wind's fair; top the bowling;
Out with the mainsail! Where's your whistle, master?

134.S.P. BROTHER] *this edn.; Daugh.*   145. all.] *Leech; Q prints* "All" *as*
Q.   *S.P. before l. 146.*
141.S.P. SECOND FRIEND] *F;* "1.*Fr.*"   146–147.] *Q lines end:* top the/your/
Q.   master.

---

132. *gelt*] castrated.
138. *if . . . in*] if he is having good luck; Tilley, H 67.
144. *tackling*] rigging.
145. *weigh*] raise the mast.
146. *top the bowling*] tighten the rope controlling the sails.

BROTHER.
    Let's get her in.
JAILER.
    Up to the top, boy!
BROTHER.   Where's the pilot?
FIRST FRIEND.   Here.
DAUGHTER.
    What kenn'st thou?
SECOND FRIEND.   A fair wood.
DAUGHTER.   Bear for it, master.   150
    Tack about!   *Sings.*
    When Cynthia with her borrowed light, etc.

                                                    Exeunt.

[IV.ii]   *Enter* Emilia *alone, with two pictures.*

EMILIA.
    Yet I may bind those wounds up, that must open
    And bleed to death for my sake else: I'll choose
    And end their strife. Two such young handsome men
    Shall never fall for me; their weeping mothers,
    Following the dead cold ashes of their sons,   5
    Shall never curse my cruelty. Good heaven,
    What a sweet face has Arcite! If wise nature,
    With all her best endowments, all those beauties
    She sows into the births of noble bodies,
    Were here a mortal woman and had in her   10
    The coy denials of young maids, yet doubtless
    She would run mad for this man. What an eye,
    Of what a fiery sparkle and quick sweetness,

150–151. Bear . . . about] *one line in*   151. Tack] *F;* take *Q.*
Q.

___

    150. *What kenn'st thou*] what can you see.
    150. *Bear for*] sail towards.
    151. *Tack about*] turn the ship round.
    152. *When . . . light*] The song in which this line occurs has not been
identified; Thomas Sackville's "Tragedy of Henry Duke of Buckingham"
in *The Mirror for Magistrates* (1563) contains the line, "And pale Cinthea
with her borrowed light" (l. 43).
[IV.ii]
    13. *quick*] lively.

Has this young prince! Here love himself sits smiling!
Just such another wanton Ganymede   15
Set Jove afire with and enforc'd the god
Snatch up the goodly boy and set him by him,
A shining constellation. What a brow,
Of what a spacious majesty, he carries,
Arch'd like the great-eyed Juno's, but far sweeter,   20
Smoother than Pelops' shoulder! Fame and honor,
Methinks, from hence, as from a promontory
Pointed in heaven, should clap their wings and sing
To all the under world the loves and fights
Of gods, and such men near 'em. Palamon   25
Is but his foil; to him, a mere dull shadow;
He's swarth and meager, of an eye as heavy
As if he had lost his mother; a still temper,
No stirring in him, no alacrity,
Of all this sprightly sharpness, not a smile.   30
Yet these that we count errors may become him:
Narcissus was a sad boy but a heavenly.
O, who can find the bent of woman's fancy?
I am a fool, my reason is lost in me,
I have no choice and I have lied so lewdly   35
That women ought to beat me. On my knees
I ask thy pardon. Palamon, thou art alone
And only beautiful, and these the eyes,
These the bright lamps of beauty, that command
And threaten love; and what young maid dare cross 'em?   40

16. Jove] *1750;* Love *Q.*

---

15. *Ganymede*] Ovid *Metamorphoses* x. 155–161.

21. *Pelops' shoulder*] the left shoulder of Pelops was made of ivory; Ovid *Metamorphoses* vi. 403–411.

23. *Pointed*] coming to a point.

25. *near*] i.e., in achievement.

26. *foil*] dull metal used behind or around a jewel to set off its brilliance by contrast.

27. *swarth*] of dark complexion.

27. *meager*] thin.

30. *this*] i.e., Arcite's.

31. *become*] suit.

32. *Narcissus*] cf. II.ii.119–121.

35. *lewdly*] ignorantly.

What a bold gravity, and yet inviting,
Has this brown manly face! O love, this only
From this hour is complexion. Lie there, Arcite:
Thou art a changeling to him, a mere gipsy,
And this the noble body. I am sotted,   45
Utterly lost; my virgin's faith has fled me;
For if my brother, but even now, had ask'd me
Whether I lov'd, I had run mad for Arcite;
Now if my sister, more for Palamon.
Stand both together. Now, come ask me, brother;   50
Alas, I know not. Ask me now, sweet sister;
I may go look. What a mere child is fancy,
That having two fair gauds of equal sweetness,
Cannot distinguish, but must cry for both!

Enter a Gentleman.

How now, sir?
GENTLEMAN.   From the noble duke, your brother,   55
    Madam, I bring you news. The knights are come.
EMILIA.
    To end the quarrel?
GENTLEMAN.   Yes.
EMILIA.   Would I might end first!
What sins have I committed, chaste Diana,
That my unspotted youth must now be soil'd
With blood of princes, and my chastity   60
Be made the altar where the lives of lovers—
Two greater and two better never yet
Made mothers joy—must be the sacrifice

54.1.] *1711; Enter Emil. and Gent. Q.*   55.] *Q prints S.P. "Emil." before this line.*

---

43. *complexion*] the only handsome color; current taste was for fair skin.
44. *changeling*] a child secretly substituted for another in infancy, therefore usually ugly.
44. *gipsy*] The normal sense, "dark-skinned," seems oddly inappropriate to Arcite, whose skin has been described as lighter than Palamon's.
46. *virgin's faith*] dedication to virginity.
48. *Whether*] which of them.
52. *I . . . look*] I am at a loss.
53. *gauds*] toys.
59. *soil'd*] defiled.
63. *joy*] rejoice.

To my unhappy beauty?

Enter Theseus, Hippolyta, Pirithous *and attendants.*

THESEUS.   Bring 'em in
Quickly, by any means; I long to see 'em.—   65
Your two contending lovers are return'd
And with them their fair knights. Now, my fair sister,
You must love one of them.
EMILIA.   I had rather both:
So neither for my sake should fall untimely.
THESEUS.
Who saw 'em?
PIRITHOUS.   I awhile.
GENTLEMAN.   And I.   70

Enter a Messenger.

THESEUS.
From whence come you, sir?
MESSENGER.   From the knights.
THESEUS.   Pray speak,
You that have seen them, what they are.
MESSENGER.   I will, sir,
And truly what I think. Six braver spirits
Than these they have brought—if we judge by the outside—
I never saw, nor read of. He that stands   75
In the first place with Arcite, by his seeming
Should be a stout man, by his face, a prince:
His very looks so say him; his complexion,
Nearer a brown than black, stern and yet noble,
Which shows him hardy, fearless, proud of dangers;   80
The circles of his eyes show fire within him,
And as a heated lion, so he looks;

64.] *Q line ends:* quickly.   76. first] *F;* fitst *Q.*
70.1.] *"Enter   Messengers.   Curtis."*   81. fire] *Dyce;* faire *Q.*
after l. 69 in Q. Cf. Intro., p. xii.

64. *unhappy*] causing misfortune.
69. *untimely*] prematurely.
77. *stout*] brave.
81. *circles . . . eyes*]? his eyeballs.
82. *heated*] angry.

His hair hangs long behind him, black and shining,
Like ravens' wings; his shoulders broad and strong;
Arm'd long and round; and on his thigh a sword   85
Hung by a curious baldric, when he frowns
To seal his will with; better, o'my conscience,
Was never soldier's friend.

THESEUS.
Thou hast well describ'd him.

PIRITHOUS.   Yet a great deal short,
Methinks, of him that's first with Palamon.   90

THESEUS.
Pray speak him, friend.

PIRITHOUS.   I guess he is a prince too,
And, if it may be, greater; for his show
Has all the ornament of honor in't.
He's somewhat bigger than the knight he spoke of,
But of a face far sweeter; his complexion   95
Is as a ripe grape ruddy. He has felt,
Without doubt, what he fights for, and so apter
To make this cause his own. In's face appears
All the fair hopes of what he undertakes,
And when he's angry, then a settled valor,   100
Not tainted with extremes, runs through his body
And guides his arm to brave things; fear he cannot,
He shows no such soft temper. His head's yellow,
Hard-hair'd and curl'd, thick twin'd, like ivy-tods,
Not to undo with thunder; in his face   105
The livery of the warlike maid appears,
Pure red and white, for yet no beard has blest him;
And in his rolling eyes sits victory,
As if she ever meant to court his valor;
His nose stands high, a character of honor;   110

86–87. baldric, . . . with;] *1750;*   104. ivy-tods] *Littledale;* Ivy tops *Q.*
Bauldricke; . . . with. *Q.*   109. court] *Littledale;* corect *Q.*

---

86. *curious baldric*] finely made shoulder strap.
86–87. *when . . . with*] to perform his purpose with when he is angry.
97. *what . . . for*] i.e., love.
104. *ivy-tods*] ivy bushes.
106. *warlike maid*] presumably Athene.
110. *character*] distinctive sign.

His red lips, after fights, are fit for ladies.

EMILIA.

Must these men die too?

PIRITHOUS.   When he speaks, his tongue
Sounds like a trumpet; all his lineaments
Are as a man would wish 'em, strong and clean;
He wears a well-steel'd axe, the staff of gold;   115
His age some five and twenty.

MESSENGER.   There's another,
A little man, but of a tough soul, seeming
As great as any; fairer promises
In such a body yet I never look'd on.

PIRITHOUS.

O, he that's freckle-fac'd?

MESSENGER.   The same, my lord: 120
Are they not sweet ones?

PIRITHOUS.   Yes, they are well.

MESSENGER.   Methinks,
Being so few and well dispos'd, they show
Great and fine art in nature. He's white-hair'd,
Not wanton white, but such a manly color
Next to an auburn; tough and nimble-set,   125
Which shows an active soul; his arms are brawny,
Lin'd with strong sinews—to the shoulder-piece
Gently they swell, like women new-conceiv'd,
Which speaks him prone to labor, never fainting
Under the weight of arms; stout-hearted, still,   130
But when he stirs, a tiger; he's gray-eyed,
Which yields compassion where he conquers; sharp
To spy advantages, and where he finds 'em,
He's swift to make 'em his; he does no wrongs,
Nor takes none; he's round-fac'd, and when he smiles   135
He shows a lover, when he frowns, a soldier;
About his head he wears the winner's oak,

---

118. *great*] large.
124. *wanton*] amorous.
124. *white*] fair; perhaps alluding to "white boy," mother's darling,
Tilley, B 579.
127. *Lin'd*] strengthened.

And in it stuck the favor of his lady;
His age, some six and thirty; in his hand
He bears a charging-staff emboss'd with silver.   140

THESEUS.

Are they all thus?

PIRITHOUS.   They are all the sons of honor.

THESEUS.

Now, as I have a soul, I long to see 'em!—
Lady, you shall see men fight now.

HIPPOLYTA.   I wish it;
But not the cause, my lord. They would show
Bravely about the titles of two kingdoms;   145
'Tis pity love should be so tyrannous.—
O my soft-hearted sister, what think you?
Weep not, till they weep blood. Wench, it must be.

THESEUS.

You have steel'd 'em with your beauty. —Honor'd friend,
To you I give the field; pray order it   150
Fitting the persons that must use it.

PIRITHOUS.   Yes, sir.

THESEUS.

Come, I'll go visit 'em: I cannot stay,
Their fame has fir'd me so, till they appear.
Good friend, be royal.

PIRITHOUS.   There shall want no bravery.

EMILIA.

Poor wench, go weep; for whosoever wins   155
Loses a noble cousin for thy sins.   *Exeunt.*

153. so, . . . appear.] *1711;* so; . . .
appeare, *Q.*

---

138. *favor*] token.
140. *charging-staff*] lance for tilting.
149. *steel'd*] made them inflexible.
150. *order*] arrange.
153. *fame*] report.
154. *royal*] lavish, generous (in preparing for the combat).
154. *want*] be lacking.
154. *bravery*] display.

[IV.iii]   *Enter* Jailer, Wooer [*and*] Doctor.

DOCTOR.

Her distraction is more at some time of the moon than at
other some, is it not?

JAILER.

She is continually in a harmless distemper, sleeps little;
altogether without appetite, save often drinking; dreaming
of another world and a better; and what broken piece of   5
matter so e'er she's about, the name Palamon lards it, that
she farces ev'ry business withal, fits it to every question.

                Enter [Jailer's] Daughter.

Look where she comes; you shall perceive her behavior.

DAUGHTER.

I have forgot it quite; the burden on't was *down-a, down-a,*
and penn'd by no worse man than Giraldo, Emilia's school-   10
master; he's as fantastical too, as ever he may go upon's
legs—for in the next world will Dido see Palamon, and then
will she be out of love with Aeneas.

DOCTOR.

What stuff's here! Poor soul.

JAILER.

E'en thus all day long.   15

DAUGHTER.

Now for this charm that I told you of; you must bring a
piece of silver on the tip of your tongue, or no ferry: then if

---

1–34.] *arranged as verse in* Q.   7.1] *Q prints after* business.

2. *other some*] others.
3. *distemper*] derangement.
5–6. *what . . . about*] whatever nonsense she is busy with.
6. *lards*] intersperses.
7. *farces*] stuffs.
9. *burden*] refrain.
9. *down-a*] very common, especially in sad songs; used in mad speeches
of Ophelia, *Hamlet*, IV.v.170, and of Lucibella in Chettle's *Tragedy of
Hoffman*, V.i.56–59.
11. *fantastical*] full of strange fancies.
12–13. *Dido . . . Aeneas*] Virgil *Aeneid* vi. 450–474, describes Dideo's
repulse of Aeneas in Hades; this passage may own something to *Antony and
Cleopatra*, IV.xiv.51–52 and V.ii.304–306.
17. *piece . . . tongue*] to pay Charon for passage in his ferry over the river
Styx.

it be your chance to come where the blessed spirits are—
there's a sight now! We maids that have our livers perish'd,
crack'd to pieces with love, we shall come there and do 20
nothing all day long but pick flowers with Proserpine;
then will I make Palamon a nosegay, then let him mark me
—then—

DOCTOR.

How prettily she's amiss! Note her a little further.

DAUGHTER.

Faith, I'll tell you; sometime we go to barley-break, we of 25
the blessed. Alas, 'tis a sore life they have i'th'other place;
such burning, frying, boiling, hissing, howling, chatt'ring,
cursing; O, they have shrewd measure; take heed! If one
be mad, or hang or drown themselves, thither they go,
Jupiter bless us, and there shall we be put in a caldron of 30
lead and usurers' grease, amongst a whole million of cut-
purses, and there boil like a gammon of bacon that will
never be enough.

DOCTOR.

How her brain coins!

DAUGHTER.

Lords and courtiers that have got maids with child, they are 35
in this place; they shall stand in fire up to the navel and
in ice up to th' heart, and there th'offending part burns
and the deceiving part freezes; in troth, a very grievous
punishment, as one would think, for such a trifle; believe
me, one would marry a leprous witch to be rid on't, I'll 40
assure you.

18 spirits are] *Mason;* spirits, as *Q*.   33.] *"Exit." after* enough *in Q*.
26. i'th'other] *F;* i'th Thother *Q*.

19–20. *livers . . . love*] The liver was thought to be the seat of violent
passion and particularly of love.
21. *Proserpine*] abducted by Pluto while gathering flowers; Ovid *Metamorphoses* v. 385–571.
25. *barley-break*] an old country game, played by couples; one couple,
being left in the middle (called "hell") had to catch the others. If a couple
separated while being chased they had to change partners. *Barley-break*
was currently used to mean "coupling."
28. *shrewd measure*] harsh punishment.
33. *enough*] thoroughly cooked.
34. *coins*] imagines.

DOCTOR.

> How she continues this fancy! 'Tis not an engraffed madness
> but a most thick and profound melancholy.

DAUGHTER.

> To hear there a proud lady and a proud city wife howl
> together! I were a beast and I'd call it good sport: one   45
> cries, "O, this smoke!" th'other, "This fire!" One cries,
> "O, that ever I did it behind the arras!" and then howls;
> th'other curses a suing fellow and her garden house.   *Sings.*
> *I will be true, my stars, my fate, etc.*   *Exit.*

JAILER.

> What think you of her, sir?   50

DOCTOR.

> I think she has a perturbed mind, which I cannot minister
> to.

JAILER.

> Alas, what then?

DOCTOR.

> Understand you she ever affected any man ere she beheld
> Palamon?   55

JAILER.

> I was once, sir, in great hope she had fix'd her liking on this
> gentleman, my friend.

WOOER.

> I did think so too, and would account I had a great pen'-
> worth on't to give half my state that both she and I, at this
> present, stood unfeignedly on the same terms.   60

---

46. th'other] *Dyce;* another *Q.*   51–89.] *arranged as verse in Q.*
47. behind] *Q (corr.);* behold
(uncorr.).

---

42. *engraffed*] deep-seated.
43. *melancholy*] literally "black bile"; used of mental states supposed
to result from its excess.
45. *and*] if.
47. *arras*] tapestry covering a wall.
48. *suing*] beseeching.
48. *garden house*] summerhouse.
49. *I . . . fate*] The song in which this line occurs has not been identified.
54. *affected*] fancied.
58–59. *would . . . on't*] would think I had a good bargain.
59. *state*] estate.

DOCTOR.

That intemperate surfeit of her eye hath distemper'd the
other senses; they may return and settle again to execute
their preordain'd faculties, but they are now in a most
extravagant vagary. This you must do: confine her to a
place where the light may rather seem to steal in than be   65
permitted. Take upon you, young sir her friend, the name
of Palamon; say you come to eat with her and to commune
of love. This will catch her attention, for this her mind beats
upon; other objects that are inserted 'tween her mind and
eye become the pranks and friskins of her madness. Sing   70
to her such green songs of love as she says Palamon hath
sung in prison; come to her stuck in as sweet flowers as
the season is mistress of, and thereto make an addition of
some other compounded odors, which are grateful to the
sense. All this shall become Palamon, for Palamon can sing   75
and Palamon is sweet and ev'ry good thing. Desire to eat
with her, carve her, drink to her, and still among intermingle
your petition of grace and acceptance into her favor. Learn
what maids have been her companions and play-feres, and
let them repair to her, with Palamon in their mouths, and   80
appear with tokens, as if they suggested for him. It is a
falsehood she is in, which is with falsehoods to be combatted.
This may bring her to eat, to sleep, and reduce what's now

---

77. carve] F; crave Q.

---

61. *intemperate*] immoderate.
61. *distemper'd*] unbalanced.
64. *extravagant*] wandering beyond their limits.
67. *commune*] talk.
68–69. *beats upon*] is obsessed by.
70. *pranks*] tricks.
70. *friskins*] frolics.
71. *green*] immature.
74. *compounded odors*] mixed perfumes.
74. *grateful*] pleasing.
77. *carve her*] carve for her at table.
77. *still among*] every now and then.
79. *play-feres*] playfellows.
81. *suggested for him*] wooed on his behalf.
81–82. *It . . . combatted*] Tilley, D 174, "One deceit drives out another."
82. *falsehood*] deception.

out of square in her into their former law and regiment.
I have seen it approved, how many times I know not, but   85
to make the number more, I have great hope in this. I will,
between the passages of this project, come in with my appliance. Let us put it in execution, and hasten the success,
which, doubt not, will bring forth comfort.   *Exeunt.*

[V.i]
    Flourish. Enter Theseus, Pirithous, *Hippolyta,* [*and*] *attendants.*

THESEUS.
    Now let 'em enter and before the gods
    Tender their holy prayers. Let the temples
    Burn bright with sacred fires and the altars
    In hallowed clouds commend their swelling incense
    To those above us: let no due be wanting.   5

               Flourish of cornets.

    They have a noble work in hand, will honor
    The very powers that love 'em.

        Enter Palamon *and* Arcite *and their knights.*

PIRITHOUS.   Sir, they enter.
THESEUS.
    You valiant and strong-hearted enemies,
    You royal german foes, that this day come
    To blow that nearness out that flames between ye,   10
    Lay by your anger for an hour and dove-like
    Before the holy altars of your helpers,
    The all-fear'd gods, bow down your stubborn bodies:
    Your ire is more than mortal; so your help be;

0.1. *Flourish*] Q *prints at end of IV.iii.*

---

  84. *out of square*] disordered.
  84. *regiment*] rule.
  85. *approved*] proved by experience.
  87. *passages*] episodes.
  87–88. *appliance*] treatment.
  88. *success*] outcome.
[V.i]
  3. *fires*] dissyllabic.
  9. *german*] closely related.
  10. *nearness*] intimacy.

And as the gods regard ye, fight with justice.   15
I'll leave you to your prayers, and betwixt ye
I part my wishes.
PIRITHOUS.   Honor crown the worthiest!

Exit Theseus, *and his train.*

PALAMON.

The glass is running now that cannot finish
Till one of us expire. Think you but thus,
That were there aught in me which strove to show   20
Mine enemy in this business, were't one eye
Against another, arm oppress'd by arm,
I would destroy th'offender; coz, I would,
Though parcel of myself. Then from this gather
How I should tender you.
ARCITE.   I am in labor   25
To push your name, your ancient love, our kindred,
Out of my memory, and i'th' selfsame place
To scat something I would confound. So hoist we
The sails, that must these vessels port even where
The heavenly limiter pleases.
PALAMON.   You speak well.   30
Before I turn, let me embrace thee, cousin.
This I shall never do again.   [*They embrace.*]
ARCITE.   One farewell.
PALAMON.

Why, let it be so: farewell, coz.
ARCITE.   Farewell, sir.

Exeunt Palamon *and his knights.*

Knights, kinsmen, lovers, yea, my sacrifices,
True worshippers of Mars, whose spirit in you   35
Expels the seeds of fear and th'apprehension

33.1.] *Q prints after* coz.

15. *regard*] are watching.
18. *glass*] hourglass.
20. *strove to show*] tried to appear.
24. *parcel*] part.
25. *tender*] esteem.
29. *port*] bring to harbor.
30. *limiter*] God, who has predestined the time and place of their deaths.
36. *apprehension*] anticipation.

Which still is further of it, go with me
Before the god of our profession. There
Require of him the hearts of lions and
The breath of tigers, yea, the fierceness too,   40
Yea, the speed also—to go on, I mean,
Else wish we to be snails. You know my prize
Must be dragg'd out of blood; force and great feat
Must put my garland on me, where she sticks,
The queen of flowers. Our intercession, then,   45
Must be to him that makes the camp a cistern
Brimm'd with the blood of men: give me your aid,
And bend your spirits towards him.   *They kneel.*
Thou mighty one, that with thy power hast turn'd
Green Neptune into purple; whose approach   50
Comets prewarn; whose havoc in vast field
Unearthed skulls proclaim; whose breath blows down
The teeming Ceres' foison; who dost pluck,
With hand armipotent, from forth blue clouds
The mason'd turrets, that both mak'st and break'st   55
The stony girths of cities; me thy pupil,
Youngest follower of thy drum, instruct this day
With military skill, that to thy laud
I may advance my streamer and by thee
Be styl'd the lord o'th' day. Give me, great Mars,   60
Some token of thy pleasure.

---

37. further of] *this edn.:* farther off   50. whose approach] *1750; not in Q.*
Q; father of *1750 conj.*   54. armipotent] *1750;* armenypo-
44. me] *Littledale conj.; not in Q.*   tent Q.

---

37. *further*] rare form of "furtherer," encourager.
39. *Require*] request.
43. *feat*] deed.
44. *garland*] prize; referring both to the victor's crown and to Emilia.
46. *camp*] battlefield.
53. *teeming*] productive.
53. *foison*] plentiful harvest.
54. *armipotent*] mighty in arms.
54. *blue clouds*] clouds of smoke.
56. *stony girths*] walls.
58. *laud*] praise.
59. *streamer*] banner.
60. *styl'd*] named.

Here they fall on their faces, as formerly, and there is heard clanging of armor, with a short thunder, as the burst of a battle, whereupon they all rise and bow to the altar.

> O great corrector of enormous times,
> Shaker of o'er rank states, thou grand decider
> Of dusty and old titles, that heal'st with blood
> The earth when it is sick, and cur'st the world　　　　65
> O'th' pleurisy of people, I do take
> Thy signs auspiciously and in thy name
> To my design march boldly. —Let us go.　　　　*Exeunt.*

    Enter Palamon *and his knights, with the former observance.*

PALAMON.

> Our stars must glister with new fire, or be
> Today extinct; our argument is love,　　　　70
> Which if the goddess of it grant, she gives
> Victory too: then blend your spirits with mine,
> You, whose free nobleness do make my cause
> Your personal hazard. To the goddess Venus
> Commend we our proceeding, and implore　　　　75
> Her power unto our party.

    Here they kneel as formerly.

> Hail, sovereign queen of secrets, who hast power
> To call the fiercest tyrant from his rage
> And weep unto a girl; that hast the might,
> Even with an eye-glance, to choke Mars's drum　　　　80
> And turn th'alarm to whispers; that canst make
> A cripple flourish with his crutch, and cure him
> Before Apollo; that mayst force the king
> To be his subject's vassal, and induce

68. design] *1711;* designe; *Q.*

61.1. *as formerly*] apparently referring to an earlier piece of action, perhaps at l. 48, for which no stage direction survives.

62. *enormous*] disordered.

64–65. *that . . . sick*] for the idea of war as a healer, see I.ii.23–24.

66. *pleurisy*] excess; an incorrect etymology derived the word from Latin *plus*, more, rather than from Greek *pleura*, side.

68.1. *with . . . observance*] see note on l. 61.1.

79. *And weep*] and to make him weep for love.

81. *alarm*] call to arms.

83. *Apollo*] god of healing.

Stale gravity to dance; the poll'd bachelor—   85
Whose youth, like wanton boys through bonfires,
Have skipp'd thy flame—at seventy thou canst catch,
And make him, to the scorn of his hoarse throat,
Abuse young lays of love. What godlike power
Hast thou not power upon? To Phoebus thou   90
Add'st flames hotter than his: the heavenly fires
Did scorch his mortal son, thine him; the huntress,
All moist and cold, some say, began to throw
Her bow away and sigh. Take to thy grace
Me, thy vow'd soldier, who do bear thy yoke   95
As 'twere a wreath of roses, yet is heavier
Than lead itself, stings more than nettles.
I have never been foul-mouth'd against thy law;
Ne'er reveal'd secret, for I knew none; would not,
Had I kenn'd all that were; I never practiced   100
Upon man's wife, nor would the libels read
Of liberal wits; I never at great feasts
Sought to betray a beauty, but have blush'd
At simp'ring sirs that did; I have been harsh
To large confessors, and have hotly ask'd them   105
If they had mothers—I had one, a woman,
And women 'twere they wrong'd. I knew a man
Of eighty winters, this I told them, who
A lass of fourteen brided. 'Twas thy power
To put life into dust: the aged cramp   110

---

91. his:] *1750; no punct. in Q.*

---

85. *poll'd*] bald.
86. *like . . . bonfires*] J. G. Frazer, *The Golden Bough* (abridged ed.,
London, 1957), ch. lxii, records the widespread practice of jumping over
the fire at spring and midsummer festivals.
87. *skipp'd*] (1) jumped over; (2) escaped.
92. *his mortal son*] Phaëton; see explanatory note on I.ii.85–87.
92–94. *the huntress . . . sigh*] alluding to the love of Diana for Endymion;
see M. Drayton, *Endymion and Phoebe.*
100. *kenn'd*] known.
100–101. *practiced Upon*] deceived.
102. *liberal*] licentious.
105. *large confessors*] boasters in public.
105. *hotly*] angrily.

Had screw'd his square foot round,
The gout had knit his fingers into knots,
Torturing convulsions from his globy eyes
Had almost drawn their spheres, that what was life
In him seem'd torture; this anatomy   115
Had by his young fair fere a boy, and I
Believ'd it was his, for she swore it was,
And who would not believe her? Brief, I am
To those that prate and have done, no companion;
To those that boast and have not, a defier;   120
To those that would and cannot, a rejoicer.
Yea, him I do not love, that tells close offices
The foulest way, nor names concealments in
The boldest language: such a one I am,
And vow that lover never yet made sigh   125
Truer than I. O then, most soft sweet goddess,
Give me the victory of this question, which
Is true love's merit, and bless me with a sign
Of thy great pleasure.

*Here music is heard [and] doves are seen to flutter. They fall again upon
their faces, then on their knees.*

O thou that from eleven to ninety reign'st   130
In mortal bosoms, whose chase is this world
And we in herds thy game, I give thee thanks
For this fair token, which, being laid unto
Mine innocent true heart, arms in assurance
My body to this business. —Let us rise   135
And bow before the goddess. (*They bow.*) Time comes on.

                                                        Exeunt.

119. companion;] *1750; no punct.*   130.] *Q repeats S.P. Pal.*
in Q.   136.S.D. *They bow.*] *Q prints after*
120. defier;] *1750; no punct. in Q.* *l. 134.*

───

111. *square*] sturdy.
111. *round*] bent with age.
113–114. *from . . . spheres*] had almost pulled the sockets from his eyes.
115. *anatomy*] skeleton.
116. *fere*] wife.
119. *prate . . . done*] kiss and tell.
122. *close offices*] secret functions.
123. *concealments*] things that should be concealed.
128. *merit*] due reward.   131. *chase*] hunting ground.

Still music of records. Enter Emilia *in white, her hair about her shoulders,*
[with] a wheaten wreath. One in white holding up her train, her hair stuck
with flowers. One before her carrying a silver hind, in which is conveyed
incense and sweet odors; which being set upon the altar, her maids standing
aloof, she sets fire to it. Then they curtsy and kneel.

EMILIA.

O sacred, shadowy, cold and constant queen,
Abandoner of revels, mute contemplative,
Sweet, solitary, white as chaste, and pure
As wind-fann'd snow, who to thy female knights   140
Allow'st no more blood than will make a blush,
Which is their order's robe; I here, thy priest,
Am humbled 'fore thine altar. O, vouchsafe,
With that thy rare green eye, which never yet
Beheld thing maculate, look on thy virgin;   145
And sacred silver mistress, lend thine ear—
Which ne'er heard scurril term, into whose port
Ne'er enter'd wanton sound—to my petition,
Season'd with holy fear. This is my last
Of vestal office; I am bride-habited,   150
But maiden-hearted; a husband I have 'pointed,
But do not know him. Out of two, I should
Choose one and pray for his success, but I
Am guiltless of election. Of mine eyes
Were I to lose one, they are equal precious,   155
I could doom neither; that which perish'd should

152. him.] *1750;* him, *Q.*   154. election.] *Dyce; no punct. in Q.*

136.1. *Still*] soft.
136.1. *records*] rare form of "recorders," flutes.
136.2. *wheaten wreath*] emblem of virginity; cf. l. 160, below; I.i.0.3, 64.
136.3. *silver hind*] an offering appropriate to Diana as goddess of hunting
and of the moon, whose metal was silver in astrology and medicine.
145. *maculate*] dirty.
147. *port*] opening.
150. *vestal office*] duty as a virgin votary of Diana.
150. *bride-habited*] dressed as a bride.
151. *'pointed*] destined.
154. *election*] choice.
156. *doom*] condemn.

Go to't unsentenc'd. Therefore, most modest queen,
He of the two pretenders that best loves me
And has the truest title in't, let him
Take off my wheaten garland, or else grant,   160
The file and quality I hold, I may
Continue in thy band.

Here the hind vanishes under the altar and in the place ascends a rose-tree,
having one rose upon it.

See what our general of ebbs and flows
Out from the bowels of her holy altar
With sacred act advances: but one rose!   165
If well inspir'd, this battle shall confound
Both these brave knights, and I, a virgin flower,
Must grow alone, unpluck'd.

Here is heard a sudden twang of instruments and the rose falls from the tree.

The flower is fall'n, the tree descends!—O mistress,
Thou here dischargest me; I shall be gather'd.   170
I think so, but I know not thine own will:
Unclasp thy mystery. —I hope she's pleas'd;
Her signs were gracious.   *They curtsy and exeunt.*

[V.ii]

          Enter Doctor, Jailer *and* Wooer, *in* [the] *habit of Palamon.*

DOCTOR.

    Has this advice I told you done any good upon her?

WOOER.

    O, very much. The maids that kept her company
    Have half persuaded her that I am Palamon.

3–6.] *arranged as prose in* Q.

---

    158. *pretenders*] claimants.
    160. *wheaten garland*] cf. 1. 136.2.
    161–162. *The file . . . band*] that I may continue in your company in
my present rank and condition, i.e., as a virgin.
    162.2. *rose*] emblem of virginity; cf. II.ii.135–137.
    166. *If*] if I am.
    166. *confound*] destroy.
    168.1. *twang*] sudden ringing sound, not necessarily of stringed instru-
ments, which are not specified in any stage direction elsewhere in the play.
    [V.ii]
    0.1. *in . . . of*] dressed as; perhaps in the costume which Palamon
has now discarded for his armor.

    Within this half-hour she came smiling to me
    And asked me what I would eat, and when I would kiss her: 5
    I told her, presently, and kiss'd her twice.

DOCTOR.
    'Twas well done; twenty times had been far better,
    For there the cure lies mainly.

WOOER.   Then she told me
    She would watch with me tonight, for well she knew
    What hour my fit would take me.

DOCTOR.   Let her do so,   10
    And when your fit comes, fit her home, and presently.

WOOER.
    She would have me sing.

DOCTOR.
    You did so?

WOOER.   No.

DOCTOR.   'Twas very ill done, then.
    You should observe her ev'ry way.

WOOER.   Alas,
    I have no voice, sir, to confirm her that way.   15

DOCTOR.
    That's all one, if ye make a noise.
    If she entreat again, do anything.
    Lie with her, if she ask you.

JAILER.   Ho there, doctor!

DOCTOR.
    Yes, in the way of cure.

JAILER.   But first, by your leave,
    I'th' way of honesty.

DOCTOR.   That's but a niceness;   20
    Ne'er cast your child away for honesty.

11.] *Q lines end:* home/ presently.

6. *presently*] at once.
8. *mainly*] entirely.
9. *watch*] stay awake.
10,11. *fit*] (1) inclination (noun); (2) supply (verb).
14. *observe*] gratify.
18. *Ho*] stop.
20. *honesty*] chastity; reputation.
20. *niceness*] folly, unnecessary scruple.

Cure her first this way, then if she will be honest,
She has the path before her.

JAILER.   Thank ye, doctor.

DOCTOR.

Pray bring her in and let's see how she is.

JAILER.

I will, and tell her her Palamon stays for her.   25
But, doctor, methinks you are i'th' wrong still.   *Exit.*

DOCTOR.   Go, go.
You fathers are fine fools: her honesty?
And we should give her physic till we find that!

WOOER.

Why, do you think she is not honest, sir?

DOCTOR.

How old is she?

WOOER.   She's eighteen.

DOCTOR.   She may be—   30
But that's all one, 'tis nothing to our purpose.
Whate'er her father says, if you perceive
Her mood inclining that way that I spoke of,
Videlicet, the *way of flesh*—you have me?

WOOER.

Yes, very well, sir.

DOCTOR.   Please her appetite,   35
And do it home; it cures her, *ipso facto*,
The melancholy humor that infects her.

WOOER.

I am of your mind, doctor.

24–27.] *Q lines end:* in/ is/ tell her/   35. Yes] *F; Yet Q.*
doctor/ still/ honesty.

22–23. *then . . . her*] perhaps alluding to the proverb "Marriage is
honorable," Tilley, M 683.
28. *And we should*] if we had to.
28. *physic*] medicine.
34. *Videlicet*] namely.
36. *home*] thoroughly.
36. *ipso facto*] "by the very act."
37. *humor*] state of mind.

DOCTOR.

> You'll find it so. She comes; pray humor her.

Enter Jailer, [Jailer's] Daughter, [*and*] *maid.*

JAILER.

> Come, your love Palamon stays for you, child,   40
> And has done this long hour, to visit you.

DAUGHTER.

> I thank him for his gentle patience;
> He's a kind gentleman and I am much bound to him.
> Did you ne'er see the horse he gave me?

JAILER.   Yes.

DAUGHTER.

> How do you like him?

JAILER.   He's a very fair one.   45

DAUGHTER.

> You never saw him dance?

JAILER.   No.

DAUGHTER.   I have, often.

> He dances very finely, very comely,
> And, for a jig, come cut and long-tail to him,
> He turns ye like a top.

JAILER.   That's fine, indeed.

DAUGHTER.

> He'll dance the morris twenty mile an hour,   50
> And that will founder the best hobbyhorse,
> If I have any skill, in all the parish;
> And gallops to the tune of *Light o' love.*
> What think you of this horse?

JAILER.   Having these virtues
> I think he might be brought to play at tennis.   55

39. humor] *1750;* honour Q.   53. tune] *1750;* turne Q.
39.1.] Q *prints after l. 38.*

---

48. *come . . . him*] whatever the competition; Tilley, C 938; *cut* = horse
with docked tail, or gelding.

50. *morris . . . hour*] perhaps alluding to Will Kemp's famous morris
dance from London to Norwich in 1600.

51. *founder*] lame.

51. *hobbyhorse*] (1) morris dancer dressed as a horse; (2) prostitute.

52. *skill*] judgment.

53. *Light o' love*] "inconstant"; dance tune; Chappell, 221–225.

DAUGHTER.

    Alas, that's nothing.

JAILER.   Can he write and read too?

DAUGHTER.

    A very fair hand, and casts himself th'acccounts
    Of all his hay and provender: that ostler
    Must rise betime that cozens him. You know
    The chestnut mare the duke has?

JAILER.   Very well.   60

DAUGHTER.

    She is horribly in love with him, poor beast,
    But he is like his master, coy and scornful.

JAILER.

    What dowry has she?

DAUGHTER.   Some two hundred bottles
    And twenty strike of oats; but he'll ne'er have her.
    He lisps in's neighing, able to entice   65
    A miller's mare.
    He'll be the death of her.

DOCTOR.   What stuff she utters!

JAILER.

    Make curtsy, here your love comes.

WOOER.   Pretty soul,
    How do ye? That's a fine maid; there's a curtsy!

DAUGHTER.

    Yours to command, i'th' way of honesty.—   70
    How far is't now to th'end o'th' world, my masters?

DOCTOR.

    Why, a day's journey, wench.

DAUGHTER.   —Will you go with me?

WOOER.

    What shall we do there, wench?

---

57. *casts . . . accounts*] reckons the expense.
59. *cozens*] cheats.
63. *bottles*] large bundles.
64. *strike*] small sheaves.
66. *miller's mare*] proverbially sober; Tilley, M 960.
70.] proverbial; Tilley, W 155.
71. *th'end o'th' world*] to which any true lover would promise to accompany his beloved.

DAUGHTER.   Why, play at stool-ball.
    What is there else to do?
WOOER.   I am content,
    If we shall keep our wedding there.
DAUGHTER.   'Tis true;   75
    For there, I will assure you, we shall find
    Some blind priest for the purpose, that will venture
    To marry us, for here they are nice and foolish;
    Besides, my father must be hang'd tomorrow,
    And that would be a blot i'th' business.   80
    Are not you Palamon?
WOOER.   Do not you know me?
DAUGHTER.
    Yes, but you care not for me; I have nothing
    But this poor petticoat and two coarse smocks.
WOOER.
    That's all one; I will have you.
DAUGHTER.   Will you surely?
WOOER.
    Yes, by this fair hand, will I.
DAUGHTER.   We'll to bed, then.   85
WOOER.
    E'en when you will.   [*Kisses her.*]
DAUGHTER.   O sir, you would fain be nibbling.
WOOER.
    Why do you rub my kiss off?
DAUGHTER.   'Tis a sweet one,
    And will perfume me finely against the wedding.
    Is not this your cousin Arcite?
DOCTOR.   Yes, sweet heart,
    And I am glad my cousin Palamon   90
    Has made so fair a choice.
DAUGHTER.   —Do you think he'll have me?

83. two] *F;* too *Q.*

---

73. *stool-ball*] game resembling cricket, played at Easter by young men
and women.
    78. *nice*] scrupulous.
    88. *against*] in preparation for.

DOCTOR.

    Yes, without doubt.

DAUGHTER.   —Do you think so too?

JAILER.   Yes.

DAUGHTER.

    We shall have many children. —Lord, how y'are grown!
    My Palamon I hope will grow too, finely,
    Now he's at liberty. Alas, poor chicken,   95
    He was kept down with hard meat and ill lodging,
    But I'll kiss him up again.

                 Enter a Messenger.

MESSENGER.

    What do you here? You'll lose the noblest sight
    That e'er was seen.

JAILER.   Are they i'th' field?

MESSENGER.   They are.

    You bear a charge there too.

JAILER.   I'll away straight.—   100
    I must e'en leave you here.

DOCTOR.   Nay, we'll go with you·
    I will not lose the sight.

JAILER.   How did you like her?

DOCTOR.

    I'll warrant you, within these three or four days
    I'll make her right again. —You must not from her,
    But still preserve her in this way.

WOOER.   I will.   105

DOCTOR.

    Let's get her in.

WOOER.   Come, sweet, we'll go to dinner,
    And then we'll play at cards.

DAUGHTER.   And shall we kiss too?

102. sight] *Dyce;* Fight *Q.*

---

    93. *Lord . . . grown*] addressed to the Doctor, whom she takes for Arcite;
he was described as less tall than Palamon at II.i.46 (Leech).

    96. *hard meat*] unpleasant food.

    100. *bear a charge*] have a duty.

    105. *preserve . . . way*] keep treating her like this.

WOOER.
    A hundred times.
DAUGHTER.   And twenty.
WOOER.   Ay, and twenty.
DAUGHTER.
    And then we'll sleep together.
DOCTOR.   Take her offer.
WOOER.
    Yes, marry, will we.
DAUGHTER.   But you shall not hurt me.   110
WOOER.
    I will not, sweet.
DAUGHTER.   If you do, love, I'll cry.   *Exeunt.*

[V.iii]
Flourish. Enter Theseus, Hippolyta, Emilia, Pirithous, *and some attendants.*

EMILIA.
    I'll no step further.
PIRITHOUS.   Will you lose this sight?
EMILIA.
    I had rather see a wren hawk at a fly
    Than this decision: ev'ry blow that falls
    Threats a brave life; each stroke laments
    The place whereon it falls and sounds more like   5
    A bell than blade. I will stay here.
    It is enough my hearing shall be punish'd
    With what shall happen, 'gainst the which there is
    No deafing but to hear, not taint my eye
    With dread sights it may shun.
PIRITHOUS.   Sir, my good lord,   10
    Your sister will no further.
THESEUS.   O, she must:
    She shall see deeds of honor in their kind,
    Which sometime show well pencil'd. Nature now

0.1. *Flourish*] Q *prints at end of*   Curtis. Cf. *Intro., p. xii.*
V.ii.   3. decision: ev'ry] *F;* decision
0.1.] *S.D. in* Q *ends:* T. *Tucke:*   ev'ry; Q.

────────────────────────────────

13. *pencil'd*] depicted in words or painting.
13. *Nature*] as opposed to art.

Shall make and act the story, the belief
Both seal'd with eye and ear. You must be present;   15
You are the victor's meed, the prize and garland
To crown the question's title.

EMILIA.   Pardon me;
If I were there, I'd wink.

THESEUS.   You must be there;
This trial is, as 'twere, i'th' night, and you
The only star to shine.

EMILIA.   I am extinct: 20
There is but envy in that light which shows
The one the other. Darkness, which ever was
The dam of horror, who does stand accurs'd
Of many mortal millions, may even now,
By casting her black mantle over both,   25
That neither could find other, get herself
Some part of a good name, and many a murder
Set off whereto she's guilty.

HIPPOLYTA.   You must go.

EMILIA.
In faith, I will not.

THESEUS.   Why, the knights must kindle
Their valor at your eye. Know, of this war   30
You are the treasure and must needs be by
To give the service pay.

EMILIA.   Sir, pardon me;
The title of a kingdom may be tried
Out of itself.

THESEUS.   Well, well, then, at your pleasure!
Those that remain with you could wish their office   35
To any of their enemies.

HIPPOLYTA.   Farewell, sister.
I am like to know your husband 'fore yourself,
By some small start of time: he whom the gods

---

14. *make and act*] create and perform.
15. *seal'd*] attested.
16. *meed*] reward.
17. *question's title*] right of the dispute, i.e., the winner.
23. *dam*] mother.
28. *Set off*] compensate for.

Do of the two know best, I pray them he
Be made your lot.   40

Exeunt Theseus, Hippolyta, Pirithous, *etc.*

EMILIA.

Arcite is gently visag'd, yet his eye
Is like an engine bent or a sharp weapon
In a soft sheath; mercy and manly courage
Are bedfellows in his visage. Palamon
Has a most menacing aspect; his brow   45
Is grav'd and seems to bury what it frowns on;
Yet sometime 'tis not so but alters to
The quality of his thoughts; long time his eye
Will dwell upon his object. Melancholy
Becomes him nobly: so does Arcite's mirth: 50
But Palamon's sadness is a kind of mirth,
So mingled as if mirth did make him sad
And sadness, merry; those darker humors that
Stick misbecomingly on others, on him
Live in fair dwelling.   55

Cornets. Trumpets sound as to a charge.

Hark how yon spurs to spirit do incite
The princes to their proof! Arcite may win me;
And yet may Palamon wound Arcite, to
The spoiling of his figure. O, what pity
Enough for such a chance? If I were by,   60
I might do hurt; for they would glance their eyes
Toward my seat, and in that motion might
Omit a ward, or forfeit an offense
Which crav'd that very time. It is much better
I am not there. O, better never born,   65
Than minister to such harm!

54. him] *1750;* them *Q.*

---

39. *know best*] know to be the best.
42. *engine bent*] gun loaded and aimed.
46. *grav'd*] deeply lined; also suggesting "full of graves."
49. *object*] thing seen.
59. *figure*] appearance.
63. *ward*] defensive move.
63. *forfeit an offense*] lose an opportunity of attacking.

Cornets. A great cry and noise within: crying "A Palamon."

Enter [a] Servant.

                              What is the chance?

SERVANT.

    The cry's "A Palamon!"

EMILIA.

    Then he has won. 'Twas ever likely:
    He look'd all grace and success and he is
    Doubtless the prim'st of men. I prithee, run   70
    And tell me how it goes.

              Shout and cornets: crying "A Palamon."

SERVANT.   Still Palamon.

EMILIA.

    Run and enquire,   [*Exit* Servant.]
                    Poor servant, thou hast lost.
    Upon my right side still I wore thy picture,
    Palamon's on the left. Why so, I know not;
    I had no end in't; else chance would have it so,   75
    On the sinister side the heart lies: Palamon
    Had the best-boding chance.

              Another cry and shout within, and cornets.

                        This burst of clamor
    Is sure the end o'th' combat.

                    Enter Servant.

SERVANT.

    They said that Palamon had Arcite's body
    Within an inch o'th' pyramid, that the cry   80
    Was general "A Palamon!" but anon
    Th'assistants made a brave redemption, and
    The two bold titlers at this instant are

66.S.D. *Cornets . . . "A Palamon"*]   *after l. 66.*
Q prints after l. 64.   77.S.D.] *Q prints after l. 75.*
66.S.D.] *Enter a* Servant] *Q prints*   78. the end] *1750;* th'end *Q.*

    69. *success*] accented on first syllable; cf. I.i.209.
    70. *prim'st*] best.
    76. *sinister*] left; accented on second syllable.
    77. *best-boding*] best-omened.
    83. *titlers*] claimants of a title.

Hand to hand at it.

EMILIA.   Were they metamorphos'd
Both into one! O why? There were no woman   85
Worth so compos'd a man: their single share,
Their nobleness peculiar to them, gives
The prejudice of disparity, value's shortness,
To any lady breathing—

Cornets. Cry within, "Arcite, Arcite."

More exulting?
Palamon still?

SERVANT.   Nay, now the sound is "Arcite."   90

EMILIA.
I prithee lay attention to the cry;
Set both thine ears to th' business.

Cornets. A great shout and cry, "Arcite, victory!"

SERVANT.   The cry is
"Arcite" and "Victory." Hark, "Arcite, victory!"
The combat's consummation is proclaim'd
By the wind instruments.

EMILIA.   Half sights saw   95
That Arcite was no babe. God's lid, his richness
And costliness of spirit look'd through him; it could
No more be hid in him than fire in flax,
Than humble banks can go to law with waters
That drift winds force to raging. I did think   100
Good Palamon would miscarry, yet I knew not
Why I did think so; our reasons are not prophets

89.S.D.] *Q prints after l. 88.*   92.S.D.] *Q prints after l. 91.*

84. *Were they*] if only they were.
86. *compos'd*] compounded.
87. *peculiar*] individual.
87–89. *gives . . . breathing*] injures any lady living with an unequal comparison and shows her lack of value.
94. *consummation*] conclusion.
96. *lid*] eyelid.
98. *No . . . flax*] proverbial; Tilley, F 255.
100. *drift*] driving.

When oft our fancies are. They are coming off.
Alas, poor Palamon!

Cornets. Enter Theseus, Hippolyta, Pirithous, Arcite *as victor, and attendants, etc.*

THESEUS.
    Lo, where our sister is in expectation,   105
    Yet quaking and unsettled. —Fairest Emily,
    The gods, by their divine arbitrament,
    Have given you this knight: he is a good one
    As ever struck at head. Give me your hands.
    Receive you her, you him; be plighted with   110
    A love that grows as you decay.
ARCITE.   Emilia,
    To buy you, I have lost what's dearest to me,
    Save what is bought; and yet I purchase cheaply,
    As I do rate your value.
THESEUS.   O loved sister,
    He speaks now of as brave a knight as e'er   115
    Did spur a noble steed. surely the gods
    Would have him die a bachelor, lest his race
    Should show i'th' world too godlike: his behavior
    So charm'd me, that methought Alcides was
    To him a sow of lead. If I could praise   120
    Each part of him to th'all I have spoke, your Arcite
    Did not lose by't; for he that was thus good
    Encounter'd yet his better. I have heard
    Two emulous Philomels beat the ear o'th' night
    With their contentious throats, now one the higher,   125
    Anon the other, then again the first,
    And by and by outbreasted, that the sense
    Could not be judge between 'em: so it far'd
    Good space between these kinsmen, till heavens did
    Make hardly one the winner. —Wear the garland   130

111. Emilia] *Colman; Emily Q.*   121. all] *1750;* all; *Q.*

119. *Alcides*] Hercules.   120. *sow*] ingot.
122. *Did not*] would not.   124. *Philomels*] nightingales.
127. *outbreasted*] excelled in singing.

With joy, that you have won. —For the subdued,
Give them our present justice, since I know
Their lives but pinch 'em: let it here be done.
The scene's not for our seeing; go we hence,
Right joyful, with some sorrow. —Arm your prize;   135
I know you will not lose her.

Flourish.

                         —Hippolyta,
I see one eye of yours conceives a tear,
The which it will deliver.

EMILIA.   Is this winning?
O all you heavenly powers, where is your mercy?
But that your wills have said it must be so,   140
And charge me live to comfort this unfriended,
This miserable prince, that cuts away
A life more worthy from him than all women,
I should and would die too.

HIPPOLYTA.   Infinite pity
That four such eyes should be so fix'd on one   145
That two must needs be blind for't.

THESEUS.   So it is.   *Exeunt.*

[V.iv]

Enter Palamon *and his* Knights *pinioned*; Jailer, *Executioner, etc.,* [*and*]
guard.

PALAMON.
There's many a man alive that hath outliv'd
The love o'th' people; yea, i'th' selfsame state
Stands many a father with his child: some comfort
We have by so considering. We expire,
And not without men's pity; to live still,   5
Have their good wishes; we prevent

136.S.D.] *Q   prints   after*   deliver   [V.iv]
l. 138.   1.S.P.] *not in Q.*
139. your] *F;* you *Q.*

---

141. *unfriended*] deprived of a friend.
    144. *I . . . would*] I ought to and would wish to.
[V.iv]
    5–6. *to live . . . wishes*] we have men's good wishes that we might stay
alive.
    6. *prevent*] anticipate.

The loathsome misery of age, beguile
The gout and rheum, that in lag hours attend
For gray approachers; we come towards the gods
Young and unwapper'd, not halting under crimes   10
Many and stale; that sure shall please the gods
Sooner than such, to give us nectar with 'em,
For we are more clear spirits. My dear kinsmen,
Whose lives for this poor comfort are laid down,
You have sold 'em too too cheap.

FIRST KNIGHT.   What ending could be   15
Of more content? O'er us the victors have
Fortune, whose title is as momentary
As to us death is certain; a grain of honor
They not o'erweigh us.

SECOND KNIGHT.   Let us bid farewell,
And with our patience anger tott'ring fortune,   20
Who at her certain'st reels.

THIRD KNIGHT.   Come, who begins?

PALAMON.
E'en he that led you to this banquet shall
Taste to you all. —Aha, my friend, my friend,
Your gentle daughter gave me freedom once;
You'll see't done now forever. Pray, how does she?   25
I heard she was not well; her kind of ill
Gave me some sorrow.

JAILER.   Sir, she's well restor'd
And to be married shortly.

PALAMON.   By my short life,
I am most glad on't; 'tis the latest thing
I shall be glad of. Prithee tell her so;   30
Commend me to her, and to piece her portion

10. unwapper'd, not] F; unwapper'd, Q.

---

8. *rheum*] catarrh.
8. *lag*] last.
8. *attend*] wait.
9. *gray approachers*] old men who approach them.
10. *unwapper'd*] unexhausted.
13. *clear*] innocent.
20. *tott'ring*] unstable.
21. *reels*] staggers.
31. *to . . . portion*] to make up her dowry; cf. IV.i.21–24.

Tender her this.   [*Gives his purse.*]

FIRST KNIGHT.   Nay, let's be offerers all.

SECOND KNIGHT.

Is it a maid?

PALAMON.   Verily, I think so;

A right good creature, more to me deserving

Than I can quite or speak of.

ALL KNIGHTS.   Commend us to her.   35

They give their purses.

JAILER.

The gods requite you all, and make her thankful.

PALAMON.

Adieu; and let my life be now as short

As my leave-taking.   *Lies on the block.*

FIRST KNIGHT.   Lead, courageous cousin.

SECOND AND THIRD KNIGHTS.

We'll follow cheerfully.

A great noise within: crying, "Run! Save! Hold!" Enter in haste a Messenger.

MESSENGER.

Hold, hold! O hold, hold, hold!   40

Enter Pirithous *in haste.*

PIRITHOUS.

Hold, ho! It is a cursed haste you made

If you have done so quickly. —Noble Palamon,

The gods will show their glory in a life

That thou art yet to lead.

PALAMON.   Can that be, when

Venus, I have said, is false? How do things fare?   45

PIRITHOUS.

Arise, great sir, and give the tidings ear,

36.] *Q prints as two lines ending:* all/   *Littledale;* "1.2. *K.*" *Q.*
thankful.   44.] *Q line ends:* be.
39.S.P. SECOND AND THIRD KNIGHTS]

32. *Tender*] offer.
33. *maid*] virgin.
35. *quite*] requite.

That are most rarely sweet and bitter.

PALAMON.   What

Hath wak'd us from our dream?

PIRITHOUS.   List, then. Your cousin,

 Mounted upon a steed that Emily
 Did first bestow on him, a black one, owing   50
 Not a hair worth of white—which some will say
 Weakens his price, and many will not buy
 His goodness with this note; which superstition
 Here finds allowance—on this horse is Arcite,
 Trotting the stones of Athens, which the calkins 55
 Did rather tell than trample; for the horse
 Would make his length a mile, if't pleas'd his rider
 To put pride in him. As he thus went counting
 The flinty pavement, dancing as 'twere to th' music
 His own hooves made—for, as they say, from iron 60
 Came music's origin—what envious flint,
 Cold as old Saturn and like him possess'd
 With fire malevolent, darted a spark,
 Or what fierce sulphur else, to this end made,
 I comment not—the hot horse, hot as fire, 65
 Took toy at this and fell to what disorder

---

47. rarely] *1750 conj.;* early Q.

50–54. *a black one . . . allowance*] horses of single unvaried color were popularly supposed to be vicious.

50. *owing*] owning.

52. *price*] value.

53. *note*] feature.

55. *calkins*] turned-down edges under horseshoe.

56. *tell*] count.

57. *make . . . mile*] "take mile-long paces" (Leech).

60–61. *from . . . origin*] alluding either to the conflation of Jubal, inventor of music, with Tubal-cain, the first metal-worker (Genesis 4:21–22); or to the tradition that Pythagoras invented music while hammering on an anvil.

62. *Saturn*] a malign planet of cold nature; Saturn causes Arcite's accident in *The Knight's Tale.*

64. *sulphur*] "In popular belief . . . associated with the fires of hell, with devils, and with thunder and lightning" (*OED*).

64. *end*] purpose.

65. *comment*] explain.

66. *Took toy*] took fright.

His power could give his will; bounds; comes on end;
Forgets school doing, being therein train'd
And of kind manage; pig-like he whines
At the sharp rowel, which he frets at rather   70
Than any jot obeys; seeks all foul means
Of boist'rous and rough jad'ry to disseat
His lord, that kept it bravely. When nought serv'd,
When neither curb would crack, girth break, nor diff'ring
    plunges
Disroot his rider whence he grew, but that   75
He kept him 'tween his legs, on his hind hooves
On end he stands,
That Arcite's legs, being higher than his head,
Seem'd with strange art to hang. His victor's wreath
Even then fell off his head; and presently   80
Backward the jade comes o'er and his full poise
Becomes the rider's load. Yet is he living;
But such a vessel 'tis that floats but for
The surge that next approaches. He much desires
To have some speech with you. Lo, he appears.   85

       Enter Theseus, Hippolyta, Emilia, Arcite *in a chair.*

PALAMON.

     O miserable end of our alliance!
     The gods are mighty.—Arcite, if thy heart,
     Thy worthy, manly heart, be yet unbroken,
     Give me thy last words. I am Palamon,
     One that yet loves thee dying.

ARCITE.   Take Emilia,   90

     And with her all the world's joy. Reach thy hand.
     Farewell; I have told my last hour. I was false,
     Yet never treacherous; forgive me, cousin.—
     One kiss from fair Emilia. [*Kisses her.*] 'Tis done:

79. victor's] *Q* (*corr.*); victoros   87. mighty.] *1750; no punct. in Q.*
(*uncorr.*).

---

72. *jad'ry*] behavior suiting a *jade*, or inferior horse.
73. *kept it bravely*] kept his seat excellently.
81. *poise*] weight.
92. *told*] counted.

Take her. I die.   [*Dies.*]
PALAMON.   Thy brave soul seek Elysium!   95
EMILIA.

    I'll close thine eyes, prince; blessed souls be with thee!
    Thou art a right good man and, while I live,
    This day I give to tears.
PALAMON.   And I to honor.
THESEUS.

    In this place first you fought; e'en very here
    I sunder'd you. Acknowledge to the gods   100
    Our thanks that you are living.
    His part is play'd and, though it were too short,
    He did it well; your day is lengthen'd, and
    The blissful dew of heaven does arrouse you.
    The powerful Venus well hath grac'd her altar,   105
    And given you your love; our master, Mars,
    Hath vouch'd his oracle and to Arcite gave
    The grace of the contention: so the deities
    Have show'd due justice. — Bear this hence.
PALAMON.   O cousin,
    That we should things desire, which do cost us   110
    The loss of our desire! That nought could buy
    Dear love, but loss of dear love!
THESEUS.   Never fortune

    Did play a subtler game: the conquer'd triumphs,
    The victor has the loss; yet in the passage
    The gods have been most equal. Palamon,   115
    Your kinsman hath confess'd the right o'th' lady
    Did lie in you; for you first saw her and
    Even then proclaim'd your fancy; he restor'd her
    As your stol'n jewel and desir'd your spirit
    To send him hence forgiven. The gods my justice   120
    Take from my hand and they themselves become
    The executioners. Lead your lady off;

---

101. Our] *Q;* Your *Dyce.*   107. Hath] *Dyce;* Hast *Q.*

104. *arrouse*] sprinkle.
106. *our master*] Theseus refers to Mars as the patron of soldiers, including
himself, Hippolyta, and Pirithous.
107. *vouch'd*] upheld.   108. *grace*] favor.
110. *desire*] trisyllabic in this line.   114. *passage*] process.

And call your lovers from the stage of death,
Whom I adopt my friends. A day or two
Let us look sadly and give grace unto   125
The funeral of Arcite, in whose end
The visages of bridegrooms we'll put on
And smile with Palamon, for whom an hour,
But one hour since, I was as dearly sorry
As glad of Arcite, and am now as glad   130
As for him sorry. O you heavenly charmers,
What things you make of us! For what we lack
We laugh, for what we have, are sorry; still
Are children in some kind. Let us be thankful
For that which is, and with you leave dispute   135
That are above our question. —Let's go off,
And bear us like the time.   *Flourish. Exeunt.*

133. sorry; still] *Mason;* sorry still,
Q.

---

123. *stage of death*] scaffold; perhaps the same structure as the altar in V.i.
137. *bear . . . time*] behave in a manner suiting the occasion.

EPILOGUE

I would now ask ye how ye like the play;
But, as it is with schoolboys, cannot say.
I am cruel fearful. Pray yet stay awhile,
And let me look upon ye. No man smile?
Then it goes hard, I see. He that has   5
Lov'd a young handsome wench, then, show his face—
'Tis strange if none be here—and, if he will,
Against his conscience let him hiss and kill
Our market. 'Tis in vain, I see, to stay ye.
Have at the worst can come, then! Now, what say ye?   10
And yet mistake me not: I am not bold:
We have no such cause. If the tale we have told—
For 'tis no other—any way content ye,
(For to that honest purpose it was meant ye)
We have our end; and ye shall have ere long,   15
I dare say, many a better to prolong
Your old loves to us. We, and all our might,
Rest at your service. Gentlemen, good night.   *Flourish.*

FINIS

Epilogue] Spoken by a boy, presumably the boy actor of either Emilia or
the Jailer's Daughter.
2. *say*] speak.
8–9. *kill . . . market*] spoil our takings.
9. *stay*] hold back.
12. *We . . . cause*] that is not our intention.
12. *tale*] story; implying that the play is not to be taken too seriously.
15. *end*] purpose.

Appendix

Chronology

Approximate years are indicated by *, occurrences in doubt by (?)

Political and Literary Events	*Life and Major Works of Shakespeare and Fletcher*

1557

John Shakespeare marries Mary Arden.*

1558
Accession of Queen Elizabeth I.
Robert Greene born.
Thomas Kyd born.

1560
George Chapman born.

1561
Francis Bacon born.

1564
Christopher Marlowe born.

William Shakespeare christened at Stratford-on-Avon, April 26.

1572
Thomas Dekker born.*
John Donne born.
Massacre of St. Bartholomew's Day.

1573
Ben Jonson born.*

1574
Thomas Heywood born.*

1576
The Theatre, the first permanent public theater in London, established by James Burbage.
John Marston born.

1577
The Curtain theater opened.
Holinshed's *Chronicles of England, Scotland and Ireland*.

Drake begins circumnavigation of the earth; completed 1580.

1578

John Lyly's *Euphues: The Anatomy of Wit.*

1579

Sir Thomas North's translation of Plutarch's *Lives.*

John Fletcher born at Rye, Sussex.

1580

Thomas Middleton born.

1582

Shakespeare marries Anne Hathaway.

1583

Philip Massinger born.

Susanna Shakespeare born.

1584

Francis Beaumont born.*

1585

Hamnet and Judith Shakespeare born.

1586

Death of Sir Philip Sidney.
John Ford born.
Kyd's *THE SPANISH TRAGEDY.*

1587

The Rose theater opened by Henslowe.
Marlowe's *TAMBURLAINE.* Part I.*
Execution of Mary, Queen of Scots.
Drake raids Cadiz.

1588

Defeat of the Spanish Armada.
Marlowe's *TAMBURLAINE,* Part II.*

1589

Greene's *FRIAR BACON AND FRIAR BUNGAY.*
Marlowe's *THE JEW OF MALTA.*

1590

Spenser's *Faerie Queene* (Books I–III) published.
Sidney's *Arcadia* published.

HENRY VI, Parts I–III,* *TITUS ANDRONICUS.*

1591

RICHARD III.

Fletcher admitted a pensioner of Bene't (Corpus Christi) College, Cambridge (?).

1592

Marlowe's *DOCTOR FAUSTUS** and *EDWARD II.**
Death of Greene.

TAMING OF THE SHREW.*
THE COMEDY OF ERRORS.*

1593

Death of Marlowe.
Theaters closed on account of plague.

LOVE'S LABOR'S LOST;* *Venus and Adonis* published.

1594

Death of Kyd.

TWO GENTLEMEN OF VERONA;* *The Rape of Lucrece* published.
Shakespeare's company becomes Lord Chamberlain's Men.
Fletcher takes Cambridge B.A. (?).

1595

The Swan theater built.
Sidney's *Defense of Poesy* published.
Raleigh's first expedition to Guiana.

ROMEO AND JULIET,* *A MIDSUMMER NIGHT'S DREAM,** *RICHARD II.*

1596

Spenser's *Faerie Queene* (Books IV–VI) published.
James Shirley born.

MERCHANT OF VENICE,* *KING JOHN.**
Hamnet Shakespeare dies.
Grant of arms to John Shakespeare.
Fletcher's father dies.

1597

Bacon's Essays (first edition).

HENRY IV, Part I.*
Shakespeare purchases New Place.

1598

Demolition of The Theatre.
Jonson's *EVERY MAN IN HIS HUMOR* (first version).
Seven books of Chapman's translation of Homer's *Iliad* published.

MUCH ADO ABOUT NOTHING,*
HENRY IV, Part II.*
Fletcher takes Cambridge M.A. (?).

1599

The Paul's Boys reopen their theater.
The Globe theater opened.
Marston's *ANTONIO AND MELLIDA,** Parts I and II.
Dekker's *THE SHOEMAKERS' HOLIDAY.**
Death of Spenser.

AS YOU LIKE IT,* *HENRY V,**
JULIUS CAESAR.*

1600

The Fortune theater built by Alleyn.
The Children of the Chapel begin
to play at the Blackfriars.

TWELFTH NIGHT *

1601

Insurrection and execution of the
Earl of Essex.
Jonson's *POETASTER*.

HAMLET, * *MERRY WIVES OF
WINDSOR*.*
John Shakespeare dies.

1602

TROILUS AND CRESSIDA.*

1603

Death of Queen Elizabeth I; acces-
sion of James VI of Scotland as
James I.
Florio's translation of Montaigne's
Essays published.
Heywood's *A WOMAN KILLED
WITH KINDNESS*.
Marston's *THE MALCONTENT*.*

*ALL'S WELL THAT ENDS
WELL*.*
Shakespeare's company becomes
the King's Men.

1604

Marston's *THE FAWN*.*
Chapman's *BUSSY D'AMBOIS*.*

MEASURE FOR MEASURE, *
OTHELLO.*

1605

Marston's *THE DUTCH COUR-
TESAN*.*
Bacon's *Advancement of Learning*
published.
The Gunpowder Plot.

KING LEAR.*
Fletcher's *WOMAN'S PRIZE*.*

1606

Jonson's *VOLPONE*.*
Tourneur's *REVENGER'S TRAG-
EDY*.*
The Red Bull theater built.
Death of John Lyly.

MACBETH.*

1607

Beaumont's *KNIGHT OF THE
BURNING PESTLE*.*
Settlement of Jamestown, Virginia.

ANTONY AND CLEOPATRA.*
Susanna Shakespeare marries John
Hall.
Jonson's *VOLPONE* published, with
commendatory verses by Fletcher.

1608

Chapman's *CONSPIRACY AND
TRAGEDY OF CHARLES, DUKE
OF BYRON*.*

CORIOLANUS, * *TIMON OF
ATHENS,* * *PERICLES*.*
Mary Shakespeare dies.

John Milton born.

1609
Jonson's *EPICOENE.*
Dekker's *Gull's Hornbook* published.

1610
Jonson's *ALCHEMIST.*
Chapman's *REVENGE OF BUSSY D'AMBOIS.**
Richard Crashaw born.

1611
Authorized (King James) Version of the Bible published.
Middleton's *A CHASTE MAID IN CHEAPSIDE.**
Tourneur's *ATHEIST'S TRAGEDY.**
Chapman's translation of *Iliad* completed.

1612
Webster's *THE WHITE DEVIL.**

1613
Webster's *THE DUCHESS OF MALFI.**
Sir Thomas Overbury murdered.

1614
The Globe theater rebuilt.
The Hope theater built.
Jonson's *BARTHOLOMEW FAIR.*

1615

Fletcher's *FAITHFUL SHEPHERDESS.**
Richard Burbage leases Blackfriars theater for King's Men.

*CYMBELINE;** *Sonnets* published.
Beaumont and Fletcher's *PHILASTER,** *COXCOMB.** They begin to write together for the King's Men.*

Shakespeare settles in Stratford.*
Beaumont and Fletcher's *CAPTAIN,** *MAID'S TRAGEDY.**

*THE WINTER'S TALE,** *THE TEMPEST.** Beaumont and Fletcher's *A KING AND NO KING.*

Fletcher and Shakespeare's *CARDENIO* (?).*
Fletcher marries Joan Herring (?).

The Globe theater burned.
Shakespeare's *HENRY VIII* (with Fletcher).
Fletcher and Shakespeare's *THE TWO NOBLE KINSMEN.*
Shakespeare purchased Blackfriars Gate-House.
Beaumont and Fletcher's *THE SCORNFUL LADY.**
Fletcher, Field, and Massinger's *HONEST MAN'S FORTUNE.*

Fletcher's *WIT WITHOUT MONEY.**

Fletcher's *MONSIEUR THOMAS.**

1616
Publication of Folio edition of Jonson's *Works*.
Chapman's *Whole Works of Homer*.
Death of Beaumont.

Judith Shakespeare marries Thomas Quiney, February 10.
Shakespeare revises his will, March 25.
Death of Shakespeare, April 23.
Fletcher's *MAD LOVER.**

1617

Fletcher's *CHANCES.**

1618
Outbreak of Thirty Years War.
Execution of Raleigh.

Fletcher's *LOYAL SUBJECT.**

1619

Fletcher and Massinger's *SIR JOHN VAN OLDEN BARNAVELT.*
Fletcher's *HUMOROUS LIEU-TENANT.**

1620
Settlement of Plymouth, Massa-chusetts.

Fletcher and Massinger's *CUSTOM OF THE COUNTRY,** *FALSE ONE.**

1621
Middleton's *WOMEN BEWARE WOMEN.**
Robert Burton's *Anatomy of Melan-choly* published.
Andrew Marvell born.

Fletcher and Massinger's *DOUBLE MARRIAGE.**
Fletcher's *PILGRIM,** *WILD GOOSE CHASE.**

1622
Middleton and Rowley's *THE CHANGELING.**
Henry Vaughan born.

Fletcher and Massinger's *PROPH-ETESS, SPANISH CURATE, SEA VOYAGE.*

1623

Publication of Folio edition of Shakespeare's *COMEDIES, HIS-TORIES, AND TRAGEDIES.*
Anne Shakespeare dies.
Fletcher and Massinger's *LITTLE FRENCH LAWYER.**
Fletcher and Rowley's *MAID IN THE MILL.*

1624

Fletcher's *RULE A WIFE AND HAVE A WIFE, A WIFE FOR A MONTH.*

1625
Death of King James I; accession of Charles I.

Revival of *THE TWO NOBLE KINSMEN* (?).*

Fletcher's *FAIR MAID OF THE INN* (with Massinger, Webster and Ford).
Death of Fletcher, buried August 29.

1626
Death of Tourneur.
Death of Bacon.

1627
Death of Middleton.

1628
Ford's *THE LOVER'S MELAN-CHOLY*.
Petition of Right.
Buckingham assassinated.

1631
Shirley's *THE TRAITOR*.
Death of Donne.
John Dryden born.

1632
Massinger's *THE CITY MADAM*.*

1633
Donne's *Poems* published.
Death of George Herbert.

1634
Death of Chapman, Marston, Webster.*
Milton's *Comus*.

THE TWO NOBLE KINSMEN published.

1635
Sir Thomas Browne's *Religio Medici*.

1637
Death of Jonson.

1639
First Bishops' War.
Death of Carew.*

1640
Short Parliament.
Long Parliament impeaches Laud.
Death of Massinger, Burton.

1641
Irish rebel.
Death of Heywood.

1642
Charles I leaves London; Civil War breaks out.
Shirley's *COURT SECRET*.

All theaters closed by Act of Parliament.

1643
Parliament swears to the Solemn League and Covenant.

1645
Ordinance for New Model Army enacted.

1646
End of First Civil War.

1647
Army occupies London.
Charles I forms alliance with Scots.

Publication of Folio edition of Beaumont and Fletcher's *COMEDIES AND TRAGEDIES.*

1648
Second Civil War.

1649
Execution of Charles I.

1650
Jeremy Collier born.

1651
Hobbes' *Leviathan* published.

1652
First Dutch War began (ended 1654).
Thomas Otway born.

1653
Nathaniel Lee born.*

1656
D'Avenant's *THE SIEGE OF RHODES* performed at Rutland House.

1657
John Dennis born.

1658
Death of Oliver Cromwell.
D'Avenant's *THE CRUELTY OF THE SPANIARDS IN PERU* performed at the Cockpit.

1660
Restoration of Charles II.
Theatrical patents granted to Thomas Killigrew and Sir William D'Avenant, authorizing them to form, repectively, the King's and the Duke of York's Companies.

1661
Cowley's *THE CUTTER OF COLEMAN STREET*.
D'Avenant's *THE SIEGE OF RHODES* (expanded to two parts).

1662
Charter granted to the Royal Society.

1663
Dryden's *THE WILD GALLANT*.
Tuke's *THE ADVENTURES OF FIVE HOURS*.

1664
Sir John Vanbrugh born.
Dryden's *THE RIVAL LADIES*.
Dryden and Howard's *THE INDIAN QUEEN*.
Etherege's *THE COMICAL REVENGE*.

1665
Second Dutch War began (ended 1667).
Great Plague.
Dryden's *THE INDIAN EMPEROR*.
Orrery's *MUSTAPHA*.

1666
Fire of London.
Death of James Shirley.